Harvard
Business
Review

ON

MANUFACTURING EXCELLENCE

AT TOYOTA

THE HARVARD BUSINESS REVIEW PAPERBACK SERIES

The series is designed to bring today's managers and professionals the fundamental information they need to stay competitive in a fast-moving world. From the preeminent thinkers whose work has defined an entire field to the rising stars who will redefine the way we think about business, here are the leading minds and landmark ideas that have established the *Harvard Business Review* as required reading for ambitious businesspeople in organizations around the globe.

Other books in the series:

Harvard Business Review Interviews with CEOs

Harvard Business Review on Advances in Strategy

Harvard Business Review on Appraising Employee Performance

Harvard Business Review on Becoming a High Performance Manager

Harvard Business Review on Brand Management

Harvard Business Review on Breakthrough Leadership

Harvard Business Review on Breakthrough Thinking

Harvard Business Review on Bringing Your Whole Self to Work

Harvard Business Review on Building Personal and Organizational Resilience

Harvard Business Review on the Business Value of IT

Harvard Business Review on Change

Harvard Business Review on Compensation

Harvard Business Review on Corporate Ethics

Harvard Business Review on Corporate Governance

Harvard Business Review on Corporate Responsibility

Harvard Business Review on Corporate Strategy

Harvard Business Review on Crisis Management

Harvard Business Review on Culture and Change

Harvard Business Review on Customer Relationship Management

Other books in the series (continued):

Harvard Business Review

ON

MANUFACTURING

EXCELLENCE

AT TOYOTA

A HARVARD BUSINESS REVIEW PAPERBACK

The Harvard Business Review articles in this collection are available as
individual reprints. Discounts apply to quantity purchases. For information and ordering, please contact Customer Service, Harvard Business
School Publishing, Boston, MA 02163. Telephone: (617) 783-7500 or
(800) 988-0886, 8 A.M. to 6 P.M. Eastern Time, Monday through Friday.
Fax: (617) 783-7555, 24 hours a day. E-mail: custserv@hbsp.harvard.edu.

Library of Congress cataloging information forthcoming
ISBN 978-1-4221-7977-2

Contents

Harvard Business Review

ON

MANUFACTURING EXCELLENCE AT TOYOTA

Lessons from Toyota's Long Drive

An Interview with Katsuaki Watanabe

THOMAS A. STEWART AND ANAND P. RAMAN

Executive Summary

LAST DECEMBER the Toyota Motor Corporation officially forecast that it would sell 9.34 million cars in 2007—which could make it the world's largest automaker. However, rapid growth and globalization have created many pressures for the company, and the strain of success is already beginning to show. Two HBR editors interviewed Toyota's president, Katsuaki Watanabe, and several top executives to learn about the strategies they're developing to cope in the future.

For well over a decade, J. D. Power and other research firms have consistently rated Toyotas among the top automobiles for quality, reliability, and durability. But in 2006 a series of problems with its cars threatened to sully the company's reputation. What's more, speedy expansion to meet demand and the struggle to keep pace with technological change have combined to challenge Toyota's grand ambitions and its famed "Toyota Way."

For Watanabe, being number one means "being the best in the world in terms of quality." If Toyota's quality continues to improve, he says, volume and revenues will follow. If problems arise from overstretching, he wants them made visible, because then his people will "rack their brains" to solve them—and if that means postponing growth, so be it.

Toyota's long-term strategy involves developing both global and regional car models in order to compete worldwide with a full line of products. Watanabe aims to achieve his goals through a combination of *kaizen* ("continuous improvement") and *kakushin* ("radical innovation"). One of his visions for the future is a "dream car": a vehicle that cleans the air, prevents accidents, promotes health, evokes excitement, and can drive around the world on a single tank of gas.

Toyota's way is to measure everything—even the noise that car doors make when they open and close as workers perform their final inspections on newly manufactured automobiles. By any measure, whether esoteric or mundane, Toyota Motor Corporation has become one of the most successful companies in the world today. This year marks the 70th anniversary of Toyota's founding, 50 years since the Japanese company started exporting cars to the United States, and a decade since it launched the world's first commercial hybrid, the Prius. If, as Toyota officially forecast last December, it sells 9.34 million vehicles in 2007, it will overtake America's General Motors to become the world's biggest automobile manufacturer.

Toyota is, arguably, already the best carmaker on the planet. For almost 15 years J. D. Power and other research firms have consistently rated Toyota and its luxury line, Lexus, among the top automotive brands in terms of reliability, initial quality, and long-term durability. Toyota is also the most profitable car manufacturer: In the financial year that ended in March 2007, it made a profit of $13.7 billion, whereas GM and Ford reported losses of $1.97 billion and $12.61 billion, respectively, in 2006. In fact, Toyota's market capitalization on May 10, 2007–of $186.71 billion–was more than one and a half times GM's ($16.60 billion), Ford's ($15.70 billion), and DaimlerChrysler's ($81.77 billion) combined.

In the history of the modern corporation, Toyota's march to the top from its humble beginnings as a textile machinery manufacturer in the mill town of Koromo–now Toyota City–is one of the most remarkable examples ever of managing for the long term. Toyota's rise wasn't quick or inevitable. Even in the early 1980s Ford and GM marketed bigger, better-looking, and plusher cars than Toyota did–although its soulless creations were more reliable and fuel efficient. The Japanese manufacturer closed the gap little by little, improvement by improvement. In 1970 GM had a 40% chunk of the U.S. car and light-trucks market, whereas Toyota had only a 2% sliver. Toyota's market share inched up to 3% in 1980, to 8% in 1990, and to 9% in 2000, entering double digits for the first time only in 2006, when it rose to 13% and GM's fell to 26%. Toyota's ascension is best captured by the Japanese word jojo: "slowly, gradually, and steadily."

Every executive has two questions about Toyota today: What can my company learn from the world's greatest manufacturer? and (sotto voce) How is Toyota handling success? The answer to the former is obvious (plenty), but the jury is still out on the latter. Toyota is more confident than ever in some ways. The company is proud of the fact that its management principles are different from those taught in B-schools. Senior executives take great pleasure in explaining that other companies find it difficult to emulate Toyota because its management tools matter less than its mind-set. To some observers, the company has become insufferable. For instance, after it unveiled the Lexus LS600h L at the New York Auto Show in April 2006, the influential blogger Peter DeLorenzo complained, "The tone, the language, and everything about the presentation confirmed to me that the 'creeping' arrogance that has been brewing at Toyota for years has finally blossomed into full bloom for everyone to see."

A long and deep look at Toyota, especially in Japan, reveals a different picture. The company appears to be running scared. Toyota's executives were blindsided last year by a series of problems with its automobiles that blemished the company's reputation for manufacturing quality products. They are worried about always being the second (or the sixth, according to the 2006 Formula One standings) to enter new markets and to incorporate new technologies in vehicles. They are also gravely concerned about not having enough people to sustain their global growth. In fact, almost every aspect of Toyota is straining to keep pace with the company's rapid expansion and with technological change.

These pressures are compounded by three factors. First, in order to meet demand, Toyota has added the capacity to produce 3 million automobiles over the past six years. Perhaps the only other automaker to boost production that fast, according to industry experts, was the Ford Motor Company, under Henry Ford in the early 1900s. Second, Toyota's ambitions have dramatically expanded. The company wants to develop Lexus into a big luxury brand in Europe, attacking European carmakers' biggest source of profits; to grow sales of its full-size pickup truck, the Tundra, in the United States, thereby assaulting American automakers' last redoubt; and to develop a new breed of vehicles for emerging markets such as China and India. Third, the rate of technological change both in manufacturing processes and in products is unprecedented. For instance, Toyota's vision is to develop "dream cars" that are revolutionary in safety and environmental benignity.

A series of interviews with Katsuaki Watanabe, Toyota's 65-year-old president, and several executive vice presidents revealed that Toyota's future will depend on its ability to strike the right balance—between the short term and the long term; between being a Japanese company and being a global company; between the manufacturing culture of Toyota City and the design culture of Los Angeles, where some of Toyota's cars take shape; between the cautiousness of Toyota's veterans, who are worried about growing too fast, and the confidence of its youngsters, who have seen only success. And Watanabe, who is using the Toyota Way to remake the company, told HBR's editor, Thomas A. Stewart, and senior editor Anand P. Raman that Toyota must also balance incremental improvements with radical reform. What follows is an edited version of our interview with the company's president that incorporates (and identifies) some comments by Toyota executive vice presidents.

Mr. Watanabe, you have spoken recently about how the early part of the twenty-first century is Toyota's "second founding period," when the company will set a course that will create a more prosperous society in the future. Almost in the same breath, you spoke about "fixing the foundations" of the company. Is Toyota poised for long-term growth, or does the company face a crisis?

Toyota must keep growing even as it builds a stronger foundation for the future; it has to do both for the company's long-term health. There are three keys to building a stronger foundation: We must improve product quality, keep reducing costs, and, in order to attain those two objectives, develop human resources. We have to create a stronger foundation at every stage of the supply chain, from product development to after-sales service. Our products must be the best in the world; we must be the first to offer them to customers; we must manufacture them at the lowest cost; and we must sell them through the best service networks. My focus is on how Toyota can achieve all those things at the same time.

What does becoming number one in the global automobile industry mean to you?

To me, becoming number one isn't about being the world leader in terms of how many automobiles we manufacture or sell in a year, or about generating the most sales revenues or profits. Being number one is about being the best in the world in terms of quality on a sustained basis. I attach the greatest value and importance to quality; that lies at the root of my management style. It's critical for Toyota to keep making the highest-quality vehicles in the world—the best products in every way, manufactured without any defects. Unless we enhance quality today, we can't hope for growth in the future. That's why we are investing in the development of new technologies, new processes, and human resources. My top priority is to ensure that we do that resolutely, sure-footedly, and in a thorough fashion. We've never tried to become number one in terms of volumes or revenues; as long as we keep improving our quality, size will automatically follow.

That's an ambitious agenda. But there are several pressures operating on Toyota right now. For instance, between 2004 and 2006 the company recalled more vehicles than ever before. When you took over as CEO in June 2005, you talked openly about "big-company disease" and the risks of complacency. How do you manage the tensions that growth and globalization have created?

Since I became CEO, Toyota has continued to grow very rapidly. We produced around 3 million more cars in 2006 than we did in 2000. We opened about a dozen new facilities during that period, and we are building five more plants. In 1995 there were 26 Toyota factories; in 2007 there will be 63. I've personally visited our new manufacturing facilities in China and the United States and seen the new plants we're building in Thailand, Canada, China, and Russia. Sure, every Toyota plant faces distinct challenges and difficulties, but I realize that our system may be overstretched.

We must make that issue visible. Hidden problems are the ones that become serious threats eventually. If problems are revealed for everybody to see, I will feel reassured. Because once problems have been visualized, even if our people didn't notice them earlier, they will rack their brains to find solutions to them.

That's the DNA we've all inherited through the Toyota Production System. What are the problems with the new models we have launched? Have we trained our new workers well enough to produce quality? Are our new facilities operating all right? What would be the most appropriate way of marketing and selling the Tundra, given market conditions in the United States? As long as we know what needs and challenges we face, we can come up with countermeasures.

If there are problems that go beyond our immediate capability to deal with them, we must stop if necessary, postponing projects and growth. When I drive, I have my hands on the steering wheel but I also constantly think about when I should apply the accelerator and when I should brake. I may not need to brake right now, but if a time comes at Toyota when I need to put my foot on the brake pedal rather than on the accelerator, I won't hesitate to do so.

When a Toyota worker on the shop floor notices a problem, he or she has the freedom to pull the andon *cord immediately, stop the line, and ensure that the problem is fixed before restarting production. But is it really possible to do that with the entire company? Don't you have to fix things as you go along?*

The same principle applies to management, too, and it's my job to pull the andon cord. Soon after I became president, as you know, we confronted several quality-related problems. We created teams specializing in different areas and instructed them to analyze the root causes of problems in each area. We found that in several cases the problems had occurred because of design flaws or because of short lead times that didn't allow our engineers to build a sufficient number of physical prototypes. If we had thought about product designs more clearly or had the time to conduct more experiments, we could have avoided those problems.

To prevent more problems, I suggested that we extend the deadlines for several projects by six months, even if that meant delays in new launches, and that we postpone or eliminate other projects. Of course, we couldn't delay some critical projects; we kept our eyes on market conditions and technology trends and invested additional resources to tackle problems related to those projects first. But I will not allow the same problems to recur; we won't use half-baked ideas to tackle half-cooked problems. We have to improve quality even if I have to slow our pace of growth. After examining every project in our pipeline, product by product, market by market, we have created a new product-development plan. Some projects have taken a different direction, and I have halted others—just as workers stop the line.

As Toyota's president, you have a responsibility to the capital markets. As you expand faster around the globe, will the variability of its share price—the company's beta—increase? How does Toyota address that risk in strategic terms?

The priority of Toyota's top management team is to increase shareholder value steadily over the long term. As the company continues to expand outside Japan, we will increasingly face market risk, which will vary from country to country. To create a company that can resist fluctuations all over the world all the time is difficult.

However, we use the concept of leveling fluctuations (*heijunka*), which is part of the Toyota Production System, to reduce risk. For example, the conditions in some Asian markets, such as Taiwan and Indonesia, are still tough. Japan's economy is doing better, but the automobile market is stagnant except for the minivehicles [whose engines have less than 660 cc capacity] segment. There will always be such vicissitudes in different markets, so leveling out those peaks and troughs is impor-

---

The Long-Term Growth Strategy

In 2006 Toyota President Katsuaki Watanabe unveiled the full extent of Toyota's ambitions. The company strategy puts equal emphasis on taking in opportunities and avoiding or absorbing risks; it utilizes global car models and also regional models. With global models such as the Lexus, the Camry, and the Corolla, and regional models such as the Crown (Asia) and the Tundra (North America), Toyota will offer a full line of appropriate vehicles in all the world's markets.

	Japan	North America	Europe	Asia	Others
Premium	◄——————————————Lexus——————————————►				
Large	◄—Crown—►	◄—Avalon—►		◄—Crown—►	
Medium	◄—————————————Prius————————————►				
	◄—Mark X—►		◄—Avensis—►	◄—Reiz—►	
	◄——————————————— Camry ———————————————►				
Compact		◄—Scion—►			
		◄—Matrix—►			
	◄——————————————Corolla——————————————►				
	◄—————Vitz/Yaris—————►			◄——Vios——►	
			◄—Model for Emerging Markets—►		
Truck	◄—Alphard—►	◄—Sienna—►	◄———Hilux, Innova, Fortuner———►		
SUV	◄—Estima—►	◄—Tundra—►			
Minivan	◄—————RAV4—————►				

tant. Our basic philosophy is to produce vehicles where customers are. When there are short-term demand fluctuations in one market, we use our operations in Japan to support them.

The more plants Toyota builds in different countries, the stabler its finances will become, because the company will be able to hedge against fluctuations in the yen vis-à-vis euros, dollars, and other currencies. But will your long-term strategy, which you have described as having a full line of products and competing in all regions, maintain stability? GM competes with a full line in all markets, but the strategy has proved to be more of a liability than an opportunity.

We will create a full line of appropriate products for every region in the world by offering global models and also developing regional models. In Japan we must continue to maintain our market share by launching new products that create new market segments and by revamping our sales channels. In North America we recently entered the full-size pickup truck segment with the redesigned Tundra, and we must engage more closely with Generation Y customers through brands such as the Scion. In Europe we will expand and strengthen the lineup by marketing diesel engine and hybrid vehicles. As I said earlier, we believe in building vehicles where we sell them, so we will increase our production capacity overseas.

However, that can sometimes create inflexibility in terms of capacity utilization, because local demand will fluctuate. To increase efficiency, we have developed a global link production system. Owing to the innovative technologies in our plants in Japan, we are able to transfer the production of different models between them quickly. So we have linked some plants in Japan to our overseas plants. When there is a spike in demand in, say, Europe, our plant in England will maintain stable production while the link plant in Japan manufactures the extra units needed. This system helps us in several ways: It enables us to respond swiftly to changes in demand; it enables high capacity utilization at all plants; and it saves capital expenditure, because we use existing resources in Japan to balance demand in other markets. Our plants in Japan serve as buffers, which is why our "full line, all regions" strategy works efficiently.

Japan, where you have 40% of the automobile market, is your arena for experiments with new products and production processes, and in North America and Europe, where you have 12% and 6% market shares, you plan to deepen penetration to achieve scale and profitability. But what is Toyota's vision for BRIC—Brazil, Russia, India, and China? Are they merely sources of raw materials, or are they also markets? Haven't you entered them very late?

Brazil, Russia, India, and China are entirely new markets for us. They are going to be important markets for Toyota eventually. As those economies grow, we need to figure out what kinds of manufacturing facilities we should set up and what sorts of products we need to sell. We will introduce global and regional models and augment our production bases in those countries. I don't think we are too late. Those countries are growth markets, and they will continue to grow. We don't want to be too aggressive in them despite their potential. As our former executive vice president Mr. Yoshimi Inaba said, we would not like to create large capacities and slash the price of products—as some of our rivals do—when demand doesn't pick up as anticipated. As people in BRIC look for better cars, as roads are built, and as energy efficiency becomes more important, the demand for Toyota's cars will go up. We would do better to wait than to jump into the market; we should let the market come to us. Toyota can never be a cheap brand; it's a quality product with a fair price, which in emerging markets may be a premium price. But people will see the value of our products and think, "The next time, I must buy something better—like a Toyota." We may not necessarily be somebody's first car; we definitely want to be the second car that the family buys. We should go slowly and steadily into those markets, ensuring that we stay abreast of their growth but don't go faster than is warranted.

Does the fear that Toyota may have to compromise on quality prevent you from entering the emerging markets more aggressively? Those markets demand low-priced vehicles, which embody cost-quality trade-offs that Toyota may not want to make. Is quality proving to be the enemy of growth?

It's wrong to think of the emerging markets as a single entity. Brazil is different from China, which is different from India, and so on. In Brazil the Corolla sells well; in Russia the Lexus sells extremely well. Sometimes I wonder if it's right for such an expensive car to be selling so well in Russia. Anyway, it would be wrong to say that these markets want lower-quality products. But yes, one factor they have in common is that many of their consumers want low cost automobiles. The moment I became president, I created a team to work on a project related to that. But I told our engineers, let us not focus on developing low-cost automobiles;

let us develop technologies and processes that will allow Toyota to manufacture all our vehicles at lower costs. If we do that, we can produce cars for BRIC and we can use the same processes to reduce the cost of automobiles for other countries, too. By conceptualizing the problem in that fashion, we will also meet our quality standards rather than worrying about whether we have to compromise on them in emerging markets. We have started developing those technologies already. Our rivals may be trying to create low-cost vehicles for emerging markets, but Toyota will go beyond that and develop the optimal vehicles for all worlds.

Toyota is clearly trying to grow as it has always grown, at a steady pace. But the forces of the global market are pulling you, and you are being pushed to move faster and faster to keep up. Are those forces so strong that they might pull Toyota apart? How are they changing the company's fundamental operating principles?

The Toyota Way has been and will continue to be the standard for everyone who works for Toyota all over the world. Our guiding principles define Toyota's mission and values, but the Toyota Way defines how we work. To me, it's like the air we breathe. The Toyota Way has two main pillars: continuous improvement and respect for people. Respect is necessary to work with people. By "people" we mean employees, supply partners, and customers. "Customer first" is one of the company's core tenets. We don't mean just the end customer; on the assembly line the person at the next workstation is also your customer. That leads to teamwork. If you adopt that principle, you'll also keep analyzing what you do in order to see if you're doing things perfectly, so you're not trou-

bling your customer. That nurtures your ability to identify problems, and if you closely observe things, it will
lead to *kaizen:* continuous improvement. The root of
the Toyota Way is to be dissatisfied with the status quo;
you have to ask constantly, "Why are we doing this?"
People can apply these concepts throughout the world,
not just in Japan. The question is how long it takes to
train people to develop the Toyota mind-set.

*How long does it take, especially if someone isn't Japa-
nese, to learn the Toyota Way?*

Just yesterday I spent a whole day with 30 of our young
executives. At least 50% of them were from outside
Japan. They had been broken up into teams to tackle different problems, and they made presentations based on
what they had learned about using the Toyota Way to
tackle them. I listened and commented. The managers
felt happy and said that they had learned a lot. When I
asked, many of them said they were now able to understand the Toyota Way fully. That's totally wrong. Two or
three months isn't a long enough period for anyone to
understand the Toyota Way. The managers may have
understood what's on the surface, but what lies beneath
is far greater. I asked them to explore that. There's no
end to the process of learning about the Toyota Way. I
don't think I have a complete understanding even today,
and I have worked for the company for 43 years.

*How will Toyota balance demand for its products with
the longer-term need for human resources? Making
cars is a capital-intensive business, but manufacturing
at Toyota is a human capital-intensive business. Your*

executive vice presidents all say that Toyota is facing a serious shortage of trained people. Will you be able to catch up and keep up with the demand for people?

Our demand for people is complicated by many factors that are peculiar to the automobile industry: long product life cycles; large and complex supplier networks; and, increasingly, state-of-the-art technologies vis-à-vis safety, the environment, and traveling comfort. As our executive vice president Mr. Mitsuo Kinoshita said, we need a workforce that is both specialized in new technologies and global because of Toyota's expansion. It takes time to develop Toyota people, who are trained on the job rather than in a classroom. Only when employees start working at Toyota do they learn from their superiors what values and skills they need in order to do their jobs. Most of our plants outside Japan were set up in the past ten years, so even senior employees overseas have relatively little experience with the Toyota Way.

Toyota develops T-type people. [See "Introducing T-Shaped Managers," by Morten T. Hansen and Bolko von Oetinger, HBR March 2001.] As you may know, the vertical stroke of the T stands for the fact that employees must intensify or deepen what they do, and the horizontal stroke indicates that they must learn other jobs. Creating T-type personnel is a time-consuming process. However, in many countries outside Japan it's tough to employ people for the long term. The moment we start operations, employee turnover begins. So we are learning how to retain people.

We used to transmit the Toyota Way through the mother plant system, whereby a Japanese plant served as the parent of each new overseas plant we set up. That Japanese plant was responsible for training people in the overseas plant and instilling the Toyota Way in them. Because of the rate at which we are growing overseas, we have done away with that system. We now send people from Japan, coordinators, to instill our philosophy and concepts in our overseas companies. When a new company is established, the coordinator will serve as a teacher, or *sensei,* for its employees. After some years a second-generation coordinator will serve as a coach rather than a mentor. After several more years a third-generation coordinator will act as an adviser rather than a coach. The coordinators are critical to training people in the Toyota Way, but we have only about 2,000 coordinators. Our people in Japan take turns serving as coordinators every three to five years. Given the size of our business, we need three times as many coordinators as we have at present.

As you try to keep the learning curve rising as fast as the demand curve for people, how long will it take you to triple the number of coordinators?

It's difficult to say. We spent many years developing our human resources to be able to create 2,000 coordinators. Training a T-type manager takes 20 years or so, as Toyota's executive vice president Mr. Tokuichi Uranishi told you. In addition to knowing the Toyota Production System and the Toyota Way, a coordinator needs communication skills, the ability to sense other people's feelings, and a willingness to work across cultures.

We have taken several steps to cope with the situation. First, we formally documented the Toyota Way. We had communicated its principles orally for decades, but six years ago we decided to write it down so that it could serve as a bible for overseas executives. They also use it as a measurement tool to see where they stand and how they can improve. If we hadn't planned to expand outside Japan so aggressively, we might never have written down the Toyota Way. Second, Toyota retains Japanese employees who are over 60 years old if they wish to continue to work. If they don't want to work overseas, we use them locally, and that frees younger people to serve abroad. Third, we created several new training facilities. In 2002 we set up the Toyota Institute to train executives in the Toyota Way. The institute runs a global leadership school, which develops executives from all over the world for our businesses, and a management development school, which trains our people in the application of the Toyota Way. We also set up a global production center in Japan in 2003, which you visited, and regional centers in Thailand, the United States, and the UK. These centers "train the trainers" in plant management techniques, management roles, and shop-floor skills.

Finally, some of our overseas affiliates, such as Toyota Canada and Toyota Kentucky, have close to 20 years' experience with the Toyota Way. The time has come to send employees from those companies to serve as coordinators, especially to other English-speaking markets. This will be the first time we will be using non-Japanese employees to train other non-Japanese employees. There is a sense of urgency in the company, and we should be able to develop enough people to sustain the pace of our global expansion.

You described the importance of kaizen, continuous improvement, in speaking about the Toyota Way. But we heard on this visit, for the first time, that you have recently started talking about kakushin—*revolutionary change or radical innovation—as well. Is incremental improvement no longer enough in these revolutionary times?*

Fifteen years ago I would have said that as long as we had enough people, Toyota could achieve its goals through kaizen. In today's world, however, change can be produced by kaizen, but it may also need to be brought about by kakushin. When the rate of change is too slow, we have no choice but to resort to drastic changes or reform: *kaikaku.* Take the movement of parts in a factory, for example. Moving components doesn't add to their value; on the contrary, it destroys value, because parts may be dropped or scratched. So the movement of components should be limited as much as possible. I want our production engineers to take on the challenge of ensuring that things move as little as possible—close to the theoretical limit of zero—on shop floors. Doing that requires courage—and radical thinking.

Does the new manufacturing facility that Toyota is building at Takaoka incorporate the kind of radical change you think is needed?

The new manufacturing processes at Takaoka will completely change the way Toyota makes cars. We call them the "simple, slim, and speedy" production system. Right now our processes are complicated, so when a problem occurs, it is difficult to identify the cause. We've tried to make the processes at Takaoka simple, keep the facility slim, and have people close by observe the process. Simple and slim systems make it easier for people to notice abnormalities immediately.

When the first line at Takaoka opens, this summer, it will be Toyota's fastest production line, and it will cut lead times, logistics, and assembly time in half. We also hope to reduce the number of problems at each workstation by 50%. We have installed innovations in the stamping shop, the plastic molding shop, and the paint shop. For instance, instead of a transfer bar, we will use robots. That will allow the line to move 1.7 times faster than it used to. We have cut the length of the line by half. A new painting process allows us to apply three coats at the same time, without having to wait for each coat to dry. This will shorten painting times by 40%. To build in quality, we will go beyond visual inspections and use high-precision instruments to measure several parameters. The testing devices will be located at various stages of the assembly process and will provide data in real time to factory managers and suppliers.

We will have more flexibility than ever before: Each line at Takaoka will be able to produce eight different models, so the plant will produce 16 models on two lines compared with the four or five it used to produce on three lines. In the old plant we used to make 222,000 vehicles a year on each line; now we will be able to make 250,000 units on each line. Toyota needs such radical changes today.

But Toyota is struggling to maintain the basic quality of its products. Is this the right time for you to talk about radical improvements?

It is. People can use revolutionary approaches while making incremental improvements. You can do that. In fact, while trying to come up with incremental improvements, many people come up with revolutionary ideas. The two have different focuses; there's continuous change in kaizen and there's discontinuity in kakushin. I am only trying to get people to make the leap from incremental improvement to radical improvement wherever possible.

In addition to speeding up manufacturing lines, Toyota has launched a cost reduction program called Value Innovation. What is the difference between the program called Construction of Cost Competitiveness for the 21st Century, which you headed before you took over as CEO, and Value Innovation? By how much do you hope to shave costs through VI?

We started the Value Innovation program in April 2005. It goes beyond the item-based approach we used in CCC21. It tries to reduce the cost of the components we use by incorporating several parts into one integrated system and doing away with unnecessary components. Our goal is to shrink the number of components we use by half. When we try to reduce the cost of components, we start with their design and development; we don't focus on price reductions. The process requires collaboration among our supply partners and several Toyota divisions, such as design, production engineering, and purchasing. We pursue cost reduction efforts based on relationships of trust. The improvements that result from VI will strengthen the competitiveness of both Toyota and its suppliers.

Mr. Watanabe, you have said that your job is to "surface problems" and to "surface a vision of the future." How do you and Toyota plan to invent your vision of the future, the dream car?

I don't know how many years it's going to take us, but I want Toyota to come up with the dream car—a vehicle

The Advantages of Clustering

Of Toyota's 15 plants in Japan, 12—along with the manufacturing facilities of most of the company's suppliers—are located in and around sleepy Toyota City, in Aichi Prefecture, a 45-minute drive from Nagoya. Senior executives believe that the cluster not only has allowed the company to use its "just-in-time" manufacturing system but also has shaped Toyota's culture. They plan to create similar clusters overseas.

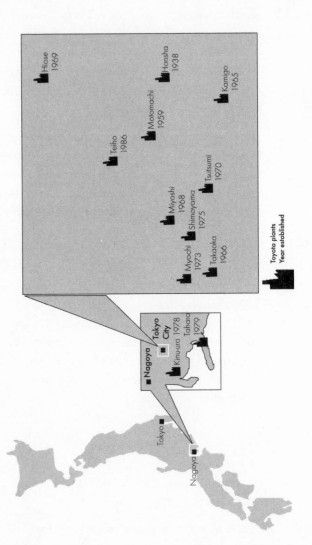

that can make the air cleaner than it is, a vehicle that cannot injure people, a vehicle that prevents accidents from happening, a vehicle that can make people healthier the longer they drive it, a vehicle that can excite, entertain, and evoke the emotions of its occupants, a vehicle that can drive around the world on just one tank of gas. That's what I dream about. We would like to develop such vehicles as quickly as possible. In my vision for the future, the most important themes are the environment, energy, safety, and evoking emotion or comfort. These are four key roads for the company's future, and we must develop technologies for each of them. Our engineers are working right now to develop the technologies we need and to incorporate them into vehicles. If we accelerate our technology development, we can realize the dream car.

As we incorporate the technologies into our vehicles, we need to study each region and match product development with the trends in each market. In Brazil, consumers can use ethanol as fuel because the country produces sugarcane. The United States is most worried about the environment and safety. We need to come up with vehicles there that use intelligent transport system technologies to satisfy consumers' requirements. In China car ownership could reach 380 million units by 2030. What will happen to petroleum prices there? What will the environmental impact be? How do we keep travelers and pedestrians safe? Energy, environment, and safety must be factored in to all the vehicles that Toyota launches in China. We refer to that as developing the right car at the right time for the right location. We need to select the appropriate fuel, technology, and supply and production system. When we combine those three elements, we will have a three-dimensional matrix. We want to produce the best cars the world has ever seen, and that, I believe, is critically important for Toyota's future.

In your two years as Toyota's president, what have you learned about being a leader?

I don't look at myself as a leader in the sense that you mean it. I have just been telling everyone in the company that we should do properly what we are trained to do. I can check how well people understand the Toyota Way in day-to-day management in any function. I visit different places to find out myself. However, my own capability and availability are limited. We have a large team of managers at Toyota, including the eight executive vice presidents, who enjoy the freedom to practice the Toyota Way in their areas of responsibility. I trust our managers to do that, but whenever there are problems, I want them to come to me with the bad news first. Other than that, my colleagues call on me to talk, to sound me out. We have hours of debate and discussion, and just as my colleagues air their opinions, I make my own views known. That's my management style. That kind of leadership is important today. Of course, we have to make decisions quickly, but we should do so steadily, thoroughly, and with an open mind. As you may have noticed, I am not afraid to do that.

Many Toyota executives talk about the importance of Toyota City in shaping the company and the values of working in a small town. Do you agree? After all, it could be argued that Detroit's provincialism is also a cause of its problems. In the Toyota of tomorrow—a company that operates out of Shanghai, Los Angeles, São Paulo, and Tokyo—how will you manage the values of Toyota's leaders and employees?

I, too, believe that the driving force behind Toyota's growth is that we are headquartered in Toyota City. We concentrate on work here and all of us tend to hold the same values. It's an excellent environment for nurturing people. Our philosophy of making things of the best possible quality has been fermented in Toyota City, which is somewhat isolated from the rest of the world. We are in the middle of nowhere; there is nothing to do but work! Toyota is the way it is because it has been nurtured in that environment. As long as we can keep that spirit— the almost crazy pursuit of quality—alive, Toyota will remain true to its values. We have been humble; that has been the traditional Toyota character. Now, of course, we constantly remind ourselves, Don't be arrogant. That's why we must train our people all over the world to understand the Toyota Way truly. We also need to gather local employees in each country in locations like Toyota City. That will allow them to soak up our concepts and mind-set. That's another priority for me: to localize our operations and to cluster them together. Thankfully, Toyota people are already transplanting these ideas throughout the world. Without those missionaries, global expansion places Toyota at a huge risk.

On the one hand, many people at Toyota make hundreds of little decisions every day to improve things. On the other hand, the company grows steadily and patiently. How do you manage these two time horizons—the quick rhythms of constant improvement and the steady rhythm of stable growth?

I don't believe the two rhythms are different. Once you indicate the direction in which the company should move, and as long as you have that direction right, you can leave other people to do the things that are necessary to get there. When people are heading in the right direction, the small movements and the major ones will stay aligned. In fact, the small changes are linked to the big changes; the people making all those small decisions together make the major movements possible. Why do you think Toyota has been successful so far? We're doing the same thing we always did; we're consistent. There's no genius in our company. We just do whatever we believe is right, trying every day to improve every little bit and piece. But when 70 years of very small improvements accumulate, they become a revolution.

The Toyota Way

TOYOTA HAS DEVELOPED distinct business beliefs and methods whose origins lie in five principles laid down in 1935 by the original company's founder, Sakichi Toyoda. However, the Toyota Way wasn't formally documented until 2001, when the company recognized that the growing number of Toyota employees outside Japan needed to be rigorously trained in its use.

In the company's own words, here are the two pillars of the Toyota Way.

I. Continuous Improvement
Challenge

WE FORM A LONG-TERM VISION, meeting challenges with courage and creativity to realize our dreams.

Kaizen *"Continuous improvement"*

WE IMPROVE OUR BUSINESS operations continuously, always driving for innovation and evolution.

Genchi genbutsu "Go and see for yourself"

WE GO TO THE SOURCE to find the facts to make correct decisions, build consensus, and achieve our goals.

II. Respect for People

Respect

WE RESPECT OTHERS, make every effort to understand each other, take responsibility, and do our best to build mutual trust.

Teamwork

WE STIMULATE PERSONAL and professional growth, share the opportunities of development, and maximize individual and team performance.

Originally published in July–August 2007
Reprint R0707E

Decoding the DNA of the Toyota Production System

STEVEN J. SPEAR AND H. KENT BOWEN

Executive Summary

THE TOYOTA PRODUCTION SYSTEM is a paradox. On the one hand, every activity, connection, and production flow in a Toyota factory is rigidly scripted. Yet at the same time, Toyota's operations are enormously flexible and responsive to customer demand. How can that be?

After an extensive four-year study of the system in more than 40 plants, the authors came to understand that at Toyota it's the very rigidity of the operations that makes the flexibility possible. That's because the company's operations can be seen as a continuous series of controlled experiments. Whenever Toyota defines a specification, it is establishing a hypothesis that is then tested through action. This approach—the scientific method—is not imposed on workers, it's ingrained in them. And it stimulates them to engage in the kind of experimentation that is widely recognized as the corner-stone of a learning organization.

The Toyota Production System grew out of the work-ings of the company over 50 years, and it has never actually been written down. Making the implicit explicit, the authors lay out four principles that show how Toyota sets up all its operations as experiments and teaches the scientific method to its workers. The first rule governs the way workers do their work. The second, the way they interact with one another. The third governs how produc-tion lines are constructed. And the last, how people learn to improve. Every activity, connection, and produc-tion path designed according to these rules must have built-in tests that signal problems immediately. And it is the continual response to those problems that makes this seemingly rigid system so flexible and adaptive to changing circumstances.

THE TOYOTA PRODUCTION SYSTEM has long been hailed as the source of Toyota's outstanding performance as a manufacturer. The system's distinctive practices— its kanban cards and quality circles, for instance—have been widely introduced elsewhere. Indeed, following their own internal efforts to benchmark the world's best man-ufacturing companies, GM, Ford, and Chrysler have inde-pendently created major initiatives to develop Toyota-like production systems. Companies that have tried to adopt the system can be found in fields as diverse as aero-space, consumer products, metals processing, and indus-trial products.

What's curious is that few manufacturers have man-aged to imitate Toyota successfully—even though the

company has been extraordinarily open about its practices. Hundreds of thousands of executives from thousands of businesses have toured Toyota's plants in Japan
and the United States. Frustrated by their inability to
replicate Toyota's performance, many visitors assume
that the secret of Toyota's success must lie in its cultural
roots. But that's just not the case. Other Japanese companies, such as Nissan and Honda, have fallen short of Toyota's standards, and Toyota has successfully introduced
its production system all around the world, including in
North America, where the company is this year building
over a million cars, mini-vans, and light trucks.

So why has it been so difficult to decode the Toyota
Production System? The answer, we believe, is that
observers confuse the tools and practices they see on
their plant visits with the system itself. That makes it
impossible for them to resolve an apparent paradox of
the system—namely, that activities, connections, and
production flows in a Toyota factory are rigidly scripted,
yet at the same time Toyota's operations are enormously
flexible and adaptable. Activities and processes are constantly being challenged and pushed to a higher level of
performance, enabling the company to continually innovate and improve.

To understand Toyota's success, you have to unravel
the paradox—you have to see that the rigid specification
is the very thing that makes the flexibility and creativity
possible. That's what we came to realize after an extensive, four-year study of the Toyota Production System in
which we examined the inner workings of more than 40
plants in the United States, Europe, and Japan, some
operating according to the system, some not. We studied
both process and discrete manufacturers whose products ranged from prefabricated housing, auto parts and

final auto assembly, cell phones, and computer printers to injection-molded plastics and aluminum extrusions. We studied not only routine production work but also service functions like equipment maintenance, workers' training and supervision, logistics and materials handling, and process design and redesign.

We found that, for outsiders, the key is to understand that the Toyota Production System creates a community of scientists. Whenever Toyota defines a specification, it is establishing sets of hypotheses that can then be tested. In other words, it is following the scientific method. To make any changes, Toyota uses a rigorous problem-solving process that requires a detailed assessment of the current state of affairs and a plan for improvement that is, in effect, an experimental test of the proposed changes. With anything less than such scientific rigor, change at Toyota would amount to little more than random trial and error—a blindfolded walk through life.

The fact that the scientific method is so ingrained at Toyota explains why the high degree of specification and structure at the company does not promote the command and control environment one might expect. Indeed, in watching people doing their jobs and in helping to design production processes, we learned that the system actually stimulates workers and managers to engage in the kind of experimentation that is widely recognized as the cornerstone of a learning organization. That is what distinguishes Toyota from all the other companies we studied.

The Toyota Production System and the scientific method that underpins it were not imposed on Toyota—they were not even chosen consciously. The system grew naturally out of the workings of the company over five decades. As a result, it has never been written down, and

Toyota's workers often are not able to articulate it. That's why it's so hard for outsiders to grasp. In this article, we attempt to lay out how Toyota's system works. We try to make explicit what is implicit. We describe four principles—three rules of design, which show how Toyota sets up all its operations as experiments, and one rule of improvement, which describes how Toyota teaches the scientific method to workers at every level of the organization. It is these rules—and not the specific practices and tools that people observe during their plant visits—that in our opinion form the essence of Toyota's system. That is why we think of the rules as the DNA of the Toyota Production System. Let's take a closer look at those rules (for a summary, see the sidebar "The Four Rules" at the end of this article).

Rule 1: How People Work

Toyota's managers recognize that the devil is in the details; that's why they ensure that all work is highly specified as to content, sequence, timing, and outcome. When a car's seat is installed, for instance, the bolts are always tightened in the same order, the time it takes to turn each bolt is specified, and so is the torque to which the bolt should be tightened. Such exactness is applied not only to the repetitive motions of production workers but also to the activities of all people regardless of their functional specialty or hierarchical role. The requirement that every activity be specified is the first unstated rule of the system. Put this baldly, the rule seems simple, something you'd expect everyone to understand and be able to follow easily. But in reality, most managers outside Toyota and its partners don't take this approach to work design and execution—even when they think they do.

Let's look at how operators at a typical U.S. auto plant install the front passenger seat into a car. They are supposed to take four bolts from a cardboard box, carry them and a torque wrench to the car, tighten the four bolts, and enter a code into a computer to indicate that the work has been done without problems. Then they wait for the next car to arrive. New operators are usually trained by experienced workers, who teach by demonstrating what to do. A seasoned colleague might be available to help a new operator with any difficulties, such as failing to tighten a bolt enough or forgetting to enter the computer code.

This sounds straightforward, so what's wrong with it? The problem is that those specifications actually allow— and even assume—considerable variation in the way employees do their work. Without anyone realizing it, there is plenty of scope for a new operator to put the seat into the vehicle differently than an experienced employee would. Some operators might put the front bolts in after the rear bolts; some might do it the other way around. Some operators might put each bolt in and then tighten them all; others might tighten as they go along. All this variation translates into poorer quality, lower productivity, and higher costs. More important, it hinders learning and improvement in the organization because the variations hide the link between how the work is done and the results.

At Toyota's plants, because operators (new and old, junior and supervisory) follow a well-defined sequence of steps for a particular job, it is instantly clear when they deviate from the specifications. Consider how workers at Toyota's Georgetown, Kentucky, plant install the right-front seat into a Camry. The work is designed as a sequence of seven tasks, all of which are expected to be completed in 55 seconds as the car moves at a fixed speed through a worker's zone. If the production worker finds himself doing task 6 (installing the rear seat-bolts) before task 4 (installing the front seat-bolts), then the job is actually being done differently than it was designed to be done, indicating that something must be wrong. Similarly, if after 40 seconds the worker is still on task 4, which should have been completed after 31 seconds, then something, too, is amiss. To make problem detection even simpler, the length of the floor for each work area is marked in tenths. So if the worker is passing the sixth of the ten floor marks (that is, if he is 33 seconds into the cycle) and is still on task 4, then he and his team leader know that he has fallen behind. Since the deviation is immediately apparent, worker and supervisor can move to correct the problem right away and then determine how to change the specifications or retrain the worker to prevent a recurrence. (See the sidebar "How Toyota's Workers Learn the Rules" at the end of this article for a short description of the process by which workers learn how to design work in this way.)

Even complex and infrequent activities, such as training an inexperienced workforce at a new plant, launching a new model, changing over a production line, or shifting equipment from one part of a plant to another, are designed according to this rule. At one of Toyota's suppliers in Japan, for example, equipment from one area of the plant was moved to create a new production line in response to changes in demand for certain products. Moving the machinery was broken into 14 separate activities. Each activity was then further subdivided and designed as a series of tasks. A specific person was assigned to do each task in a specified sequence. As each of the machines was moved, the way the tasks were actually done was compared with what was expected according to the original design, and discrepancies were immediately signaled.

In calling for people to do their work as a highly specified sequence of steps, rule 1 forces them to test hypotheses through action. Performing the activity tests the two hypotheses implicit in its design: first, that the person doing the activity is capable of performing it correctly and, second, that performing the activity actually creates the expected outcome. Remember the seat installer? If he can't insert the seat in the specified way within the specified amount of time, then he is clearly refuting at least one of these two hypotheses, thereby indicating that the activity needs to be redesigned or the worker needs to be trained.

Rule 2: How People Connect

Where the first rule explains how people perform their individual work activities, the second rule explains how they connect with one another. We express this rule as follows: every connection must be standardized and direct, unambiguously specifying the people involved, the form and quantity of the goods and services to be provided, the way requests are made by each customer, and the expected time in which the requests will be met. The rule creates a supplier-customer relationship between each person and the individual who is responsible for providing that person with each specific good or service. As a result, there are no gray zones in deciding who provides what to whom and when. When a worker makes a request for parts, there is no confusion about the supplier, the number of units required, or the timing of the delivery. Similarly, when a person needs assistance, there is no confusion over who will provide it, how the help will be triggered, and what services will be delivered.

The real question that concerns us here is whether people interact differently at Toyota than they do at other companies. Let's return to our seat installer. When he needs a new container of plastic bolt covers, he gives a request to a materials handler, who is the designated bolt-cover supplier. Commonly, such a request is made with a kanban, a laminated card that specifies the part's identification number, the quantity of parts in the container, and the locations of the part supplier and of the worker (the customer) who will install it. At Toyota, kanban cards and other devices like *andon* cords set up direct links between the suppliers and the customers. The connections are as smooth as the passing of the baton in the best Olympic relay teams because they are just as carefully thought out and executed. For example, the number of parts in a container and the number of containers in circulation for any given part are determined by the physical realities of the production system—the distances, the changeover times, and so on. Likewise, the number of workers per team is determined by the types of problems expected to occur, the level of assistance the team members need, and the skills and capabilities of the team's leader.

Other companies devote substantial resources to coordinating people, but their connections generally aren't so direct and unambiguous. In most plants, requests for materials or assistance often take a convoluted route from the line worker to the supplier via an intermediary.

The Experiments of the Toyota Production System

When organizations are managed according to the four rules, individuals are repeatedly conducting experiments, testing in operation the hypotheses built into the designs of individual work activities, customer-supplier connections, pathways, and improvement efforts. The hypotheses, the way they are tested, and the response if they are refuted are summarized below.

Rule	Hypotheses	Signs of a problem	Responses
1	The person or machine can do the activity as specified.	The activity is not done as specified.	Determine the true skill level of the person or the true capability of the machine and train or modify as appropriate.
	If the activity is done as specified, the good or service will be defect free.	The outcome is defective.	Modify the design activity.
2	Customers' requests will be for goods and services in a specific mix and volume.	Responses don't keep pace with requests.	Determine the true mix and volume of demand and the true capability of the supplier; retrain, modify activities, or reassign customer-supplier pairs as appropriate.
	The supplier can respond to customers' requests.	The supplier is idle, waiting for requests.	

3	Every supplier that is connected to the flow path is required.	A person or machine is not actually needed.	Determine why the supplier was unnecessary, and redesign the flow path.
	Any supplier not connected to the flow path is not needed.	A nonspecified supplier provides an intermediate good or service.	Learn why the nonspecified supplier was actually required, and redesign the flow path.
4	A specific change in an activity, connection, or flow path will improve cost, quality, lead time, batch size, or safety by a specific amount.	The actual result is different from the expected result.	Learn how the activity was actually performed or the connection or flow path was actually operated. Determine the true effects of the change. Redesign the change.

Any supervisor can answer any call for help because a specific person has not been assigned. The disadvantage of that approach, as Toyota recognizes, is that when something is everyone's problem it becomes no one's problem.

The requirement that people respond to supply requests within a specific time frame further reduces the possibility of variance. That is especially true in service requests. A worker encountering a problem is expected to ask for assistance at once. The designated assistant is then expected to respond immediately and resolve the problem within the worker's cycle time. If the worker is installing a front seat every 55 seconds, say, then a request for help must be answered and dealt with in less than the 55 seconds. If the problem cannot be resolved in less than 55 seconds, that failure immediately challenges the hypotheses in this customer-supplier connection for assistance. Perhaps the request signal is ambiguous. Perhaps the designated assistant has too many other requests for help and is busy or is not a capable problem solver. Constantly testing the hypotheses in this way keeps the system flexible, making it possible to adjust the system continually and constructively.

The striking thing about the requirement to ask for help at once is that it is often counterintuitive to managers who are accustomed to encouraging workers to try to resolve problems on their own before calling for help. But then problems remain hidden and are neither shared nor resolved companywide. The situation is made worse if workers begin to solve problems themselves and then arbitrarily decide when the problem is big enough to warrant a call for help. Problems mount up and only get solved much later, by which time valuable information about the real causes of the problem may have been lost.

Rule 3: How the Production Line Is Constructed

All production lines at Toyota have to be set up so that every product and service flows along a simple, specified path. That path should not change unless the production line is expressly redesigned. In principle, then, there are no forks or loops to convolute the flow in any of Toyota's supply chains. That's the third rule.

To get a concrete idea of what that means, let's return to our seat installer. If he needs more plastic bolt covers, he orders them from the specific material handler responsible for providing him with bolt covers. That designated supplier makes requests to his own designated supplier at the off-line store in the factory who, in turn, makes requests directly to his designated supplier at the bolt cover factory's shipping dock. In this way, the production line links each person who contributes to the production and delivery of the product, from the Toyota factory, through the molding company, to even the plastic pellet manufacturer.

The point is that when production lines are designed in accordance with rule 3, goods and services do not flow to the next available person or machine but to a *specific* person or machine. If for some reason that person or machine is not available, Toyota will see it as a problem that might require the line to be redesigned.

The stipulation that every product follow a simple, prespecified path doesn't mean that each path is dedicated to only one particular product, however. Quite the contrary: each production line at a Toyota plant typically accommodates many more types of products than its counterparts do at other companies.

The third rule doesn't apply only to products—it applies to services, like help requests, as well. If our seat installer, for example, needs help, that too comes from a single, specified supplier. And if that supplier can't provide the necessary assistance, she, in turn, has a designated helper. In some of Toyota's plants, this pathway for assistance is three, four, or five links long, connecting the shop floor worker to the plant manager.

The third rule runs contrary to conventional wisdom about production lines and pooling resources—even contrary to how most people think the Toyota Production System works. According to received wisdom, as a product or service is passed down the line, it should go to the next machine or person available to process it further. Similarly, most people assume that help should come from the first available person rather than from a specific person. At one auto parts supplier we studied, for example, most of the parts could be stamped on more than one press machine and welded at more than one welding station. Before the company adopted the Toyota system, its practice was to pass each part on to the first available press machine and to the first available welder. When the plant switched over, under Toyota's guidance, each type of part followed only one production path through the plant.

By requiring that every pathway be specified, the rule ensures that an experiment will occur each time the path is used. Here the hypotheses embedded in a pathway designed according to rule 3 are that every supplier connected to the pathway is necessary, and any supplier not connected is not necessary. If workers at the auto parts supplier found themselves wanting to divert production to another machine or welding station, or if they began turning for help to someone other than their designated helpers, they'd conclude that their actual demand or capacity didn't match their expectations. And there would also be no ambiguity about which press or welder was involved. Again, the workers would revisit the design of their production line. Thus rule 3, like rules 1 and 2, enables Toyota to conduct experiments and remain flexible and responsive.

Rule 4: How to Improve

Identifying problems is just the first step. For people to consistently make effective changes, they must know how to change and who is responsible for making the changes. Toyota explicitly teaches people how to improve, not expecting them to learn strictly from personal experience. That's where the rule for improvement comes in. Specifically, rule 4 stipulates that any improvement to production activities, to connections between workers or machines, or to pathways must be made in accordance with the scientific method, under the guidance of a teacher, and at the lowest possible organizational level. Let's look first at how Toyota's people learn the scientific method.

HOW PEOPLE LEARN TO IMPROVE

In 1986, Aisin Seiki, a Toyota Group company that made complex products such as power trains for the auto industry, created a line to manufacture mattresses to absorb excess capacity in one of its plants. Since 1986, its range has grown from 200 to 850 types of mattresses, its volume has grown from 160 mattresses per day to 550, and its productivity has doubled. Here's an example of how they did it.

On one of our visits to this plant, we studied a team of mattress assembly workers who were being taught to improve their problem-solving skills by redesigning their own work. Initially, the workers had been responsible for doing only their own standardized work; they had not been responsible for solving problems. Then the workers were assigned a leader who trained them to frame problems better and to formulate and test hypotheses—in other words, he taught them how to use the scientific method to design their team's work in accordance with the first three rules. The results were impressive. One of the team's accomplishments, for instance, was to redesign the way edging tape was attached to the mattresses, thereby reducing the defect rate by 90%. (See the exhibit "On-Demand Production at the Aisin Mattress Factory.")

On-Demand Production at the Aisin Mattress Factory

Aisin Seiki produces 850 varieties of mattresses, distinguished by size, firmness, covering fabric, quilting pattern, and edge trim. Customers can order any one of these in a retail store and have it delivered to their homes in three days, yet Aisin maintains an inventory at the plant equal to just 1.5 days of demand. To be able to do so, Aisin has made thousands of changes in individual work activities, in the connections linking customers and suppliers of intermediate goods and services, and to the overall production lines. This table captures how dramatic the results of those changes have been.

	1986	1988	1992	1996	1997
Styles	200	325	670	750	850
Units per day	160	230	360	530	550
Units per person	8	11	13	20	26
Productivity index	100	138	175	197	208
Finished-goods inventory (days)	30	2.5	1.8	1.5	1.5
Number of assembly lines	2	2	3	3	2

To make changes, people are expected to present the explicit logic of the hypotheses. Let's look at what that can involve. Hajime Ohba, general manager of the Toyota Supplier Support Center, was visiting a factory in which one of TSSC's consultants was leading a training and improvement activity (for a description of the role of the Toyota Production System promotion centers, see the sidebar "Toyota's Commitment to Learning" at the end of this article). The consultant was helping factory employees and their supervisor reduce the manufacturing lead time of a particular line, and Ohba was there to evaluate the group's progress.

Group members began their presentation by describing the steps by which their product was created—delineating all the problems they identified when they had first studied the process for changing over a machine from making one part to making another, and explaining the specific changes they had made in response to each of those problems. They concluded by saying, "When we started, the changeover required 15 minutes. We were hoping to reduce that by two-thirds—to achieve a five-minute changeover—so that we could reduce batch sizes by two-thirds. Because of the modifications we made, we achieved a changeover time of seven and a half minutes—a reduction of one-half."

After their presentation, Ohba asked why the group members had not achieved the five-minute goal they had originally established. They were a bit taken aback. After all, they had reduced the changeover time by 50%, yet Ohba's question suggested he had seen opportunities for even greater improvement that they had missed. They offered explanations having to do with machine complexity, technical difficulty, and equipment upgrade costs. Ohba responded to these replies with yet more questions, each one meant to push the consultant and the factory people to articulate and challenge their most basic assumptions about what could and could not be changed—assumptions that both guided and constrained the way they had solved their problems. Were they sure four bolts were necessary? Might the changeover be accomplished with two? Were they certain that all the steps they included in the changeover were needed? Might some be combined or eliminated? In asking why they had not achieved the five-minute goal, Ohba was not suggesting that the team had failed. Rather, he was trying to get them to realize that they had not fully explored all their improvement opportunities because they had not questioned their assumptions deeply enough.

There was a second reason for Ohba's persistence. He was trying to show the group members that their improvement activity had not been carried out as a bona fide experiment. They had established a goal of five minutes based on the premise that faster changeovers and smaller batches are better than slower changeovers and larger batches. But here they were confusing goals with predictions based on hypotheses. The goal was not a prediction of what they believed they would achieve through the specific improvement steps they planned to take. As a result, they had not designed the improvement effort as an experiment with an explicit, clearly articulated, verifiable hypothesis of the form, "If we make the following specific changes, we expect to achieve this specific outcome." Although they had reduced the changeover time considerably, they had not tested the hypotheses implicit in their effort. For Ohba, it was critical that the workers and their supervisor realize that how they made changes was as important as what changes they made.

WHO DOES THE IMPROVEMENT

Frontline workers make the improvements to their own jobs, and their supervisors provide direction and assistance as teachers. If something is wrong with the way a worker connects with a particular supplier within the immediate assembly area, the two of them make improvements, with the assistance of their common supervisor. The Aisin team we described earlier, for example, consisted of the assembly line workers and the supervisor, who was also their instructor. When changes are made on a larger scale, Toyota ensures that improvement teams are created consisting of the people who are directly affected and the person responsible for supervising the pathways involved.

Thus the process remains the same even at the highest levels. At Aisin's mattress factory, we found that the plant manager took responsibility for leading the change from three production lines back to two (the number had risen to three to cope with an increase in product types). He was involved not just because it was a big change but also because he had operational responsibility for overseeing the way work flowed from the feeder lines to the final assembly lines. In this way, Toyota ensures that problem solving and learning take place at all levels of the company. Of course, as we have already seen, Toyota will bring in external experts as necessary to ensure the quality of the learning process.

In the long term, the organizational structures of companies that follow the Toyota Production System will shift to adapt to the nature and frequency of the problems they encounter. Since the organizational changes are usually being made at a very low level, however, they can be hard for outsiders to detect. That's because it is the nature of the problems that determines who should solve them and how the organization is designed. One consequence is that different organizational structures coexist quite happily even in the same plant.

Consider Toyota's engine-machining plant in Kamigo, Japan. The plant has two machine divisions, each of which has three independent production shops. When we visited in summer 1998, the production people in the first machine division answered to shop heads, and the process engineers answered directly to the head of the division. However, in the second machine division, the engineers were distributed among the three shops and, like the production workers, answered to the various shop heads. Neither organizational structure is inherently superior. Rather, the people we interviewed explained, problems in the first division happened to create a situation that required the engineers to learn from one another and to pool engineering resources. By contrast, the problems that arose in the second division required the production and engineering people to cooperate at the level of the individual shops. Thus the organizational differences reflect the fact that the two divisions encountered different problems.

Toyota's Notion of the Ideal

By inculcating the scientific method at all levels of the workforce, Toyota ensures that people will clearly state the expectations they will be testing when they implement the changes they have planned. But beyond this, we found that people in companies following the Toyota Production System share a common goal. They have a common sense of what the ideal production system would be, and that shared vision motivates them to make improvements beyond what would be necessary merely to meet the current needs of their customers. This notion of the ideal is very pervasive, and we believe it is essential to understanding the Toyota Production System.

When they speak of the ideal, workers at Toyota do not mean something philosophically abstract. They have a concrete definition in mind, one that is remarkably consistent throughout the company. Very specifically, for Toyota's workers, the output of an ideal person, group of people, or machine:

- is defect free (that it, it has the features and performance the customer expects);

- can be delivered one request at a time (a batch size of one);

- can be supplied on demand in the version requested;

- can be delivered immediately;

- can be produced without wasting any materials, labor, energy, or other resources (such as costs associated with inventory); and

- can be produced in a work environment that is safe physically, emotionally, and professionally for every employee.

We consistently found people at plants that used the Toyota Production System making changes that pushed operations toward this ideal. At one company that produced electromechanical products, for example, we found that workers had come up with a number of ingenious error-detecting gauges that generated a simple, unambiguous yes-or-no signal to indicate whether their output was free of defects—as specified in the ideal. At yet another plant, which manufactures

injection-molded parts, we found that workers had
reduced the time it took to change a large molding die
from an already speedy five minutes to three minutes.
This allowed the company to reduce the batch sizes of
each part it produced by 40%, bringing it closer to the
ideal batch size of one. As Toyota moves toward the
ideal, it may temporarily hold one of its dimensions to be
more important than another. Sometimes this can result
in practices that go against the popular view of Toyota's
operations. We have seen cases where Toyota keeps
higher levels of inventory or produces in batch sizes
larger than observers generally expect of a just-in-time
operation, as we describe in the sidebar "Countermeasures in the Toyota Production System" at the end of
this article.

Toyota's ideal state shares many features of the popular notion of mass customization—the ability to create
virtually infinite variations of a product as efficiently
as possible and at the lowest possible cost. In the final
analysis, Toyota's ideal plant would indeed be one where
a Toyota customer could drive up to a shipping dock,
ask for a customized product or service, and get it at
once at the lowest possible price and with no defects.
To the extent that a Toyota plant—or a Toyota worker's
activity—falls short of this ideal, that shortcoming is
a source of creative tension for further improvement
efforts.

The Organizational Impact of the Rules

If the rules make companies using the Toyota Production System a community of scientists performing continual experiments, then why aren't these organizations
in a state of chaos? Why can one person make a change
without adversely affecting the work of other people on

the production line? How can Toyota constantly introduce changes to its operations while keeping them running at full tilt? In other words, how does Toyota improve and remain stable at the same time?

Once again, the answer is in the rules. By making people capable of and responsible for doing and improving their own work, by standardizing connections between individual customers and suppliers, and by pushing the resolution of connection and flow problems to the lowest possible level, the rules create an organization with a nested modular structure, rather like traditional Russian dolls that come one inside the other. The great benefit of nested, modular organizations is that people can implement design changes in one part without unduly affecting other parts. That's why managers at Toyota can delegate so much responsibility without creating chaos. Other companies that follow the rules will also find it possible to change without experiencing undue disruption.

Of course, the structures of other companies have features in common with those that follow the Toyota Production System, but in our research we found no company that had them all that did not follow the system. It may turn out in the end that you can build the structure only by investing the time Toyota has. But we believe that if a company dedicates itself to mastering the rules, it has a better chance of replicating Toyota's DNA—and with that, its performance.

The Four Rules

THE TACIT KNOWLEDGE that underlies the Toyota Production System can be captured in four basic rules. These rules guide the design, operation, and improvement of every activity, connection, and pathway for every product and service. The rules are as follows:

Rule 1: All work shall be highly specified as to content, sequence, timing, and outcome.

Rule 2: Every customer-supplier connection must be direct, and there must be an unambiguous yes-or-no way to send requests and receive responses.

Rule 3: The pathway for every product and service must be simple and direct.

Rule 4: Any improvement must be made in accordance with the scientific method, under the guidance of a teacher, at the lowest possible level in the organization.

All the rules require that activities, connections, and flow paths have built-in tests to signal problems automatically. It is the continual response to problems that makes this seemingly rigid system so flexible and adaptable to changing circumstances.

How Toyota's Workers Learn the Rules

IF THE RULES OF the Toyota Production System aren't explicit, how are they transmitted? Toyota's managers don't tell workers and supervisors specifically how to do their work. Rather, they use a teaching and learning approach that allows their workers to discover the rules as a consequence of solving problems. For example, the supervisor teaching a person the principles of the first rule will come to the work site and, while the person is doing his or her job, ask a series of questions:

• How do you do this work?

• How do you know you are doing this work correctly?

- How do you know that the outcome is free of defects?
- What do you do if you have a problem?

This continuing process gives the person increasingly deeper insights into his or her own specific work. From many experiences of this sort, the person gradually learns to generalize how to design all activities according to the principles embodied in rule 1.

All the rules are taught in a similar Socratic fashion of iterative questioning and problem solving. Although this method is particularly effective for teaching, it leads to knowledge that is implicit. Consequently, the Toyota Production System has so far been transferred successfully only when managers have been able and willing to engage in a similar process of questioning to facilitate learning by doing.

Toyota's Commitment to Learning

ALL THE ORGANIZATIONS WE STUDIED that are managed according to the Toyota Production System share an overarching belief that people are the most significant corporate asset and that investments in their knowledge and skills are necessary to build competitiveness. That's why at these organizations all managers are expected to be able to do the jobs of everyone they supervise and also to teach their workers how to solve problems according to the scientific method. The leadership model applies as much to the first-level "team leader" supervisors as it does to those at the top of the organization. In that way, everybody at Toyota shares in the development of human resources. In effect, there is a cascading pathway for teaching, which starts with the plant manager, that delivers training to each employee.

To reinforce the learning and improvement process, each plant and major business unit in the Toyota Group employs a number of Toyota Production System consultants whose primary responsibility is to help senior managers move their organizations toward the ideal. These "learner-leader-teachers" do so by identifying ever more subtle and difficult problems and by teaching people how to solve problems scientifically.

Many of these individuals have received intensive training at Toyota's Operations Management Consulting Division. OMCD was established in Japan as an outgrowth of efforts by Taiichi Ohno—one of the original architects of the Toyota Production System—to develop and diffuse the system throughout Toyota and its suppliers. Many of Toyota's top officers—including Toyota Motor's new president, Fujio Cho—have honed their skills within OMCD. During their OMCD tenure, which can extend for a period of years, Toyota's employees are relieved of all line responsibilities and instead are charged with leading improvement and training activities in the plants of Toyota and its suppliers. By supporting all of Toyota's plant and logistical operations in this way, OMCD serves as a training center, building its consultants' expertise by giving them opportunities to solve many difficult problems and teach others to do the same.

In 1992, Toyota founded the Toyota Supplier Support Center (TSSC) in the United States to provide North American companies with training in the Toyota Production System. Modeled on OMCD, TSSC has given workshops to more than 140 companies and direct assistance to 80. Although most of these companies are auto suppliers, few are exclusively Toyota suppliers; participants come from other industries and from universities, government organizations, and industry associations. Indeed, much of the research for this paper was derived from the experience of one of the authors, who was a member of a TSSC team for five months, promoting the Toyota Production System at a plant that supplies Toyota and two other auto assembly plants.

Countermeasures in the Toyota Production System

Toyota does not consider any of the tools or practices— such as kanbans or *andon* cords, which so many outsiders have observed and copied—as fundamental to the Toyota Production System. Toyota uses them merely as temporary responses to specific problems that will serve until a better approach is found or conditions change. They're referred to as "countermeasures," rather than "solutions," because that would imply a permanent resolution to a problem. Over the years, the company has developed a robust set of tools and practices that it uses as countermeasures, but many have changed or even been eliminated as improvements are made.

So whether a company does or does not use any particular tool or practice is no indication that it is truly applying Toyota's rules of design and improvement. In particular, contrary to the impression that the concept of zero inventory is at the heart of the Toyota system, we've observed many cases in which Toyota actually built up its inventory of materials as a countermeasure. The ideal system would in fact have no need for inventory. But, in practice, certain circumstances may require it:

- *Unpredictable downtime or yields.* Sometimes a person or a machine is unable to respond on demand when a request is made because of an unexpected mechanical breakdown. For this reason, safety stock is held to protect the customer against random occurrences. The person responsible for ensuring the reliability of a machine or process owns that inventory and strives to reduce the frequency and length of downtimes so that the amount of the safety stock can be reduced.

- *Time-consuming setups.* Difficulties in switching a machine from processing one kind of product to another can prevent a supplier from responding immediately. Therefore, suppliers will produce the product in batch sizes greater than one and hold the excess as inventory so it can respond immediately to the customer. Of course, suppliers will continually try to reduce the changeover time to keep batch sizes and stores of inventory as small as possible. Here, the owners of both the problem and the countermeasure are the machine operator and the team leader, who are responsible for reducing changeover times and batch sizes.

- *Volatility in the mix and volume of customer demand.* In some cases, variations in customers' needs are so large and unpredictable that it is impossible for a plant to adjust its production to them quickly enough. In those instances, buffer stock is kept at or near the shipping point as a countermeasure. The buffer stock also serves as a signal to production and sales managers that the person who works most directly with the customer must help that customer eliminate the underlying causes of any preventable swings in demand.

    In many cases, the same type of product is held in different types of inventory. Toyota does not pool its various kinds of inventory, even though doing so would reduce its inventory needs in the short term. That might sound paradoxical for a management system so popularly known to abhor waste. But the paradox can be resolved when we recognize that Toyota's managers and workers are trying to match each countermeasure to each problem.

There's no link between the reason for keeping safety stock—process unreliability—and the reason for keeping buffer stock—fluctuations in customer demand. To pool the two would make it hard to distinguish between the separate activities and customer-supplier connections involved. The inventory would have many owners, and the reasons for its use would become ambiguous. Pooling the inventory thus muddles both the ownership and cause of the problems, making it difficult to introduce improvements.

Originally published in September–October 1999
Reprint 99509

Learning to Lead at Toyota

STEVEN J. SPEAR

Executive Summary

MANY COMPANIES HAVE TRIED TO COPY Toyota's
famous production system—but without success. Why?
Part of the reason, says the author, is that imitators fail to
recognize the underlying principles of the Toyota Production System (TPS), focusing instead on specific tools and
practices.

This article tells the other part of the story. Building on
a previous HBR article, "Decoding the DNA of the Toyota Production System," Spear explains how Toyota
inculcates managers with TPS principles. He describes
the training of a star recruit—a talented young American
destined for a high-level position at one of Toyota's U.S.
plants. Rich in detail, the story offers four basic lessons for
any company wishing to train its managers to apply Toyota's system:

- *There's no substitute for direct observation.*
  Toyota employees are encouraged to observe

failures as they occur—for example, by sitting next to a
machine on the assembly line and waiting and watching for any problems.

- *Proposed changes should always be structured as
  experiments.* Employees embed explicit and testable
  assumptions in the analysis of their work. That allows
  them to examine the gaps between predicted and
  actual results.

- *Workers and managers should experiment as frequently as possible.* The company teaches employees at all levels to achieve continuous improvement
  through quick, simple experiments rather than through
  lengthy, complex ones.

- *Managers should coach, not fix.* Toyota managers
  act as enablers, directing employees but not telling
  them where to find opportunities for improvements.

Rather than undergo a brief period of cursory walkthroughs, orientations, and introductions as incoming fast-
track executives at most companies might, the executive
in this story learned TPS the long, hard way—by practicing it, which is how Toyota trains any new employee,
regardless of rank or function.

Toyota is one of the world's most storied companies, drawing the attention of journalists, researchers,
and executives seeking to benchmark its famous production system. For good reason: Toyota has repeatedly out-
performed its competitors in quality, reliability, productivity, cost reduction, sales and market share growth, and
market capitalization. By the end of last year it was on
the verge of replacing DaimlerChrysler as the third-
largest North American car company in terms of produc-

tion, not just sales. In terms of global market share, it has recently overtaken Ford to become the second-largest carmaker. Its net income and market capitalization by the end of 2003 exceeded those of all its competitors. But those very achievements beg a question: If Toyota has been so widely studied and copied, why have so few companies been able to match its performance?

In our 1999 HBR article, "Decoding the DNA of the Toyota Production System," H. Kent Bowen and I argued that part of the problem is that most outsiders have focused on Toyota's tools and tactics—kanban pull systems, cords, production cells, and the like—and not on its basic set of operating principles. In our article, we identified four such principles, or rules, which together ensure that regular work is tightly coupled with learning how to do the work better. These principles lead to ongoing improvements in reliability, flexibility, safety, and efficiency, and, hence, market share and profitability.

As we explained in the article, Toyota's real achievement is not merely the creation and use of the tools themselves; it is in making all its work a series of nested, ongoing experiments, be the work as routine as installing seats in cars or as complex, idiosyncratic, and large scale as designing and launching a new model or factory. We argued that Toyota's much-noted commitment to standardization is not for the purpose of control or even for capturing a best practice, per se. Rather, standardization—or more precisely, the explicit specification of how work is going to be done *before it is performed*—is coupled with testing work *as it is being done*. The end result is that gaps between what is expected and what actually occurs become immediately evident. Not only are problems contained, prevented from propagating and compromising someone else's work, but the gaps between expectations and reality are investigated; a deeper understanding of the product, process, and people is gained; and that understanding is incorporated into a new specification, which becomes a temporary "best practice" until a new problem is discovered. (See the sidebar "The Power of Principles" at the end of this article.)

It is one thing to realize that the Toyota Production System (TPS) is a system of nested experiments through which operations are constantly improved. It is another to have an organization in which employees and managers at all levels in all functions are able to live those principles and teach others to apply them. Decoding the DNA of Toyota doesn't mean that you can replicate it.

So how exactly does a company replicate it? In the following pages, I try to answer that question by describing how a talented young American, hired for an upper-level position at one of Toyota's U.S. plants, was initiated into the TPS. His training was hardly what he might have expected given his achievements. With several degrees from top-tier universities, he had already managed large plants for one of Toyota's North American competitors. But rather than undergo a brief period of cursory walkthroughs, orientations, and introductions that an incoming fast-track executive might expect, he learned TPS the long, hard way—by practicing it, which is how Toyota trains any new employee regardless of rank or function. It would take more than three months before he even arrived at the plant in which he was to be a manager.

Our American hotshot, whom we'll call Bob Dallis, arrived at the company thinking that he already knew the basics of TPS—having borrowed ideas from Toyota to improve operations in his previous job—and would simply be fine-tuning his knowledge to improve operations at his new assignment. He came out of his training realizing that improving actual operations was not *his* job—it was the job of the workers themselves. His role was to help them understand that responsibility and enable them to carry it out. His training taught him how to construct work as experiments, which would yield continuous learning and improvements, and to teach others to do the same.

The Program

Dallis arrived at Toyota's Kentucky headquarters early one wintry morning in January 2002. He was greeted by Mike Takahashi (not his real name), a senior manager of the Toyota Supplier Support Center (TSSC), a group responsible for developing Toyota's and supplier plants' competency in TPS. As such, Takahashi was responsible for Dallis's orientation into the company. Once the introductory formalities had been completed, Takahashi ushered Dallis to his car and proceeded to drive not to the plant where Dallis was to eventually work but to another Toyota engine plant where Dallis would begin his integration into the company. That integration was to involve 12 intensive weeks in the U.S. engine plant and ten days working and making observations in Toyota and Toyota supplier plants in Japan. The content of Dallis's training—as with that of any other Toyota manager—would depend on what, in Takahashi's judgment, Dallis most needed.

BACK TO BASICS

Bob Dallis's first assignment at the U.S. engine plant was to help a small group of 19 engine-assembly workers improve labor productivity, operational availability of machines and equipment, and ergonomic safety.[1] For the first six weeks, Takahashi engaged Dallis in cycles of observing and changing individuals' work processes, thereby focusing on productivity and safety. Working with the group's leaders, team leaders, and team members, Dallis would document, for instance, how different tasks were carried out, who did what tasks under what circumstances, and how information, material, and services were communicated. He would make changes to try to solve the problems he had observed and then evaluate those changes.

Dallis was not left to his own devices, despite his previous experience and accomplishments. Meetings with Takahashi bracketed his workweek. On Mondays, Dallis would explain the following: how he thought the assembly process worked, based on his previous week's observations and experiences; what he thought the line's problems were; what changes he and the others had implemented or had in mind to solve those problems; and the expected impact of his recommendations. On Fridays, Takahashi reviewed what Dallis had done, comparing actual outcomes with the plans and expectations they had discussed on Monday.

In the first six weeks, 25 changes were implemented to individual tasks. For instance, a number of parts racks were reconfigured to present materials to the operators more comfortably, and a handle on a machine was repositioned to reduce wrist strain and improve ergonomic safety. Dallis and the rest of the group also made 75 recommendations for redistributing their work. These were more substantial changes that required a reconfiguration of the work area. For instance, changing the place where a particular part was installed required relocating material stores and moving the light curtains, along with their attendant wiring and computer coding. These changes were made with the help of technical specialists from the maintenance and engineering departments while the plant was closed over the weekend, after Dallis's fifth week.

Dallis and Takahashi spent Dallis's sixth week studying the group's assembly line to see if the 75 changes actually had the desired effects. They discovered that worker productivity and ergonomic safety had improved significantly, as shown in the exhibit "The U.S. Engine Plant Assembly Line—Before and After." Unfortunately,

---

The U.S. Engine Plant Assembly Line—Before and After

The following table describes the impact of the changes Dallis made to the U.S. engine plant assembly line during his first six weeks there. He made substantial improvements in productivity—reducing the number of workers and cycle times. He and the group also made significant improvements in safety (eliminating four processes and improving the rest). But machine availability actually decreased during the period from 90% to 80%. In Dallis's second six weeks, he and his team were able to restore availability back to 90%, but this was still below the 95% target.

	Before	After
Productivity		
Number of operators	19	15
Cycle time	34 seconds	33 seconds
Total work time/engine	661 seconds	495 seconds
Ergonomics*		
Red processes	7	1
Yellow processes	2	2
Green processes	10	12
Operational availability	⊕90%	⊕80%

* Processes were rated from worst (red) to best (green) on the basis of their ergonomics—a formula that took into account weight lifted, reaching, twisting, and other risk factors.

the changes had also reduced the operational availability of the machines. This is not to say that the changes that improved productivity and ergonomics made the machines malfunction more often. Rather, before the changes were made, there was enough slack in the work so that if a machine faulted, there was often no consequence or inconvenience to anyone. But with Dallis's changes, the group was able to use 15 people instead of 19 to accomplish the same amount of work. It was also able to reduce the time required for each task and improve workload balance. With a much tighter system, previously inconsequential machine problems now had significant effects.

After Dallis had improved the human tasks in the assembly line, Takahashi had him switch to studying how the machines worked. This took another six weeks, with Takahashi and Dallis again meeting on Mondays and Fridays. Takahashi had Dallis, holder of two master's degrees in engineering, watch individual machines until they faulted so that he could investigate causes directly. This took some time. Although work-method failures occurred nearly twice a minute, machine failures were far less frequent and were often hidden inside the machine.

But as Dallis observed the machines and the people working around them, he began to see that a number of failures seemed to be caused by people's interactions with the machines. For instance, Dallis noticed that as one worker loaded gears in a jig that he then put into the machine, he would often inadvertently trip the trigger switch before the jig was fully aligned, causing the apparatus to fault. To solve that problem, Dallis had the maintenance department relocate the switch. Dallis also observed another operator push a pallet into a machine.

After investigating several mechanical failures, he realized that the pallet sometimes rode up onto a bumper in the machine. By replacing the machine's bumper with one that had a different cross-section profile, he was able to eliminate this particular cause of failure. Direct observation of the devices, root-cause analysis of each fault, and immediate reconfiguration to remove suspected causes raised operational availability to 90%, a substantial improvement though still below the 95% target that Takahashi had set for Dallis.

THE MASTER CLASS

After 12 weeks at the U.S. engine plant, Takahashi judged that Dallis had made progress in observing people and machines and in structuring countermeasures as experiments to be tested. However, Takahashi was concerned that Dallis still took too much of the burden on himself for making changes and that the rate at which he was able to test and refine improvements was too slow. He decided it was time to show Dallis how Toyota practiced improvements on its home turf. He and Dallis flew to Japan, and Dallis's first three days there were spent working at Toyota's famous Kamigo engine plant—where Taiichi Ohno, one of the main architects of TPS, had developed many of his major innovations. On the morning of their arrival, Takahashi unleashed the first of several surprises: Dallis was to work alongside an employee in a production cell and was to make 50 improvements—actual changes in how work was done—during his time there. This worked out to be one change every 22 minutes, not the one per day he had been averaging in his first five weeks of training.

The initial objective set for Dallis was to reduce the "overburden" on the worker—walking, reaching, and other efforts that didn't add value to the product and tired or otherwise impeded the worker and lengthened cycle times. Dallis's workmate could not speak English, and no translator was provided, so the two had to learn to communicate through the physical environment and through models, drawings, and role-playing. Afterward, Dallis speculated that the logic of starting with "overburden" was to get buy-in from the worker who was being asked to do his regular job while being interrupted by a non-Japanese-speaking stranger. There is also semantic significance in the phrasing: Focusing on "overburden" emphasizes the impact of the work design on the person. By contrast, focusing on "waste" suggests that the person is the problem.

Dallis applied the approach he had learned at the U.S. engine plant. On day one, he spent the first three hours observing his new workmate, and by the shift's end proudly reported that he had seven ideas, four of which he and his workmate had implemented. Then Takahashi unleashed his next surprise: He told Dallis that two Japanese team leaders who were going through the same training—people with jobs far less senior than the one for which Dallis was being prepared—had generated 28 and 31 change ideas, respectively, within the same amount of time. Somewhat humbled, Dallis picked up the pace, looking for more opportunities to make improvements and trying even more "quick and dirty" methods of testing ideas: bolting rather than welding things, taping rather than bolting, and holding rather than taping—anything to speed up the rate of feedback. By 11 AM on the second day, he and his coworker had built the list to 25 ideas. Takahashi would visit the machine shop while they were working, ask what Dallis was concentrating on, and then follow up with very specific queries about the change idea. "Before I could give a speculative answer," recalled Dallis, "he sent me to look or try for myself."

Dallis found that his ability to identify and resolve problems grew with practice, and by the morning of the third day, he had moved from examining the details of individual work routines to looking at problems with how the production cell as a whole was laid out and the effects on workers' physical movements: "There were two machines, with gauges and parts racks. A tool change took eight steps on one and 24 on the other. Was there a better layout that would reduce the number of steps and time? We figured out how to simulate the change before getting involved with heavy machinery to move the equipment for real," Dallis said. By the time the three days were up, he had identified 50 problems with quality checks, tool changes, and other work in his machine shop—35 of which had been fixed on the spot. (The effects of these changes are summarized in the exhibit "The Kamigo Report Card.")

Takahashi had Dallis conclude his shopfloor training by presenting his work to the plant manager, the machine shop manager, and the shop's group leaders. Along the way, Dallis had been keeping a careful log of the changes and their effects. The log listed operations in the shop, the individual problems Dallis had observed, the countermeasure for each problem, the effect of the change, and the first- and second-shift workers' reactions to the countermeasure. (For a snapshot of the log, see the exhibit "Excerpts from Dallis's Log.") Photographs and diagrams complemented the descriptions. "During the presentations,"

The Kamigo Report Card

During his three days at Kamigo's machining shop, Dallis documented the effects of the 50 changes he made to work motion (the physical movements of assembly-line workers) and cell layout. The changes are categorized according to the nature of the activity—walking, reaching, or other movements. They cut about half a mile of walking per shift per operator in addition to reducing ergonomic and safety hazards.

	Quality checks*			Tool changes*			Other work
	Walking	Reaching	Other	Walking	Reaching	Other	
Number of changes	8	8	13	7	4	5	5
Effect of changes	20-meter reduction (50%) per check	2-meter reduction in reaching	Elimination of tripping risk, organization of tools to reduce risk of confusion	50-meter reduction per tool	180-cm reduction in reaching	Improvement of ergonomics, organization to reduce risk of confusion	Elimination of tripping risk, simplification of oil change

* Quality checks were performed two to three times an hour, and tool changes were made once an hour.

Excerpts from Dallis's Log

Throughout his training, Dallis kept a precise log of identified problems, proposed solutions, expected results, and actual outcomes. Records like the one below are essential to the Toyota Production System, as they help encourage the precision that is necessary for true experimentation. The following excerpt shows two of the problems Dallis identified. Note that he obtained approval of his changes from the people actually doing the work. That's because at the end of the day, the people doing the work must own the solution. This kind of hierarchical inversion is a common feature of Toyota operations.

Problem #	Location	Description	Countermeasure	Result	Date	Shift 1 approval	Shift 2 approval
4	Station 6R	Team member walks 4 meters to get and then return first-piece check gauge during tool changes	Move first-piece check gauge from table to shelf between stations 5 and 6	4-meter reduction in walk/tool change	May 8	Yes	Yes
58	Part gauging area	Team member walks 5 steps to return cams to return chute, walking around light pole	Remove light pole (obstruction) and move part gauge 45Y	Reduce walk 2 steps	Not done	Yes (Pending help from maintenance department)	Yes

Dallis reported, "the plant's general manager, the machine shop's manager, and its group leaders were engaged in what [I and the other] 'lowly' team leaders said. Two-thirds [of the audience] actively took notes during the team leaders' presentations, asking pointed questions throughout."

After Dallis made his presentation, Takahashi spent the remaining week showing him how Toyota group leaders—people responsible for a few assembly or machining teams, each with three to seven members—managed and presented their improvement projects. In one case, a group leader was exploring ways of reducing machine changeover times and establishing a more even production pace for an injection-molding process. In another, a group leader was looking for ways to reduce downtime in a machining operation. In all the presentations, the group leaders explained the problems they were addressing, the processes they used to develop countermeasures, and the effect these countermeasures had on performance. Dallis quickly realized that people at all levels, even those subordinate to the one for which he was being developed, were expected to structure work and improvements as experiments.

Lessons Learned

Although Takahashi at no point told Dallis exactly what he was supposed to learn from his experience, the methodology of the training just described is so consistent and specific that it reveals at least four fundamental principles underlying the system. Together with the rules we described in our 1999 article, the following lessons may help explain why Toyota has remained the world's preeminent manufacturer.

LESSON 1

THERE'S NO SUBSTITUTE FOR DIRECT OBSERVATION.

Throughout Dallis's training, he was required to watch employees work and machines operate. He was asked not to "figure out" why a machine had failed, as if he were a detective solving a crime already committed, but to sit and wait until he could directly observe its failure—to wait for it to tell him what he needed to know.

One of the group leader presentations at Kamigo described this principle in action. In a project to improve machine maintenance, it became clear to the group that machine problems were evident only when failures occurred. In response, the shop's group leaders had removed opaque covers from several machines so that operators and team leaders could hear and see the inner workings of the devices, thus improving their ability to assess and anticipate problems with the machines. This is a very different approach from the indirect observation on which most companies rely—reports, interviews, surveys, narratives, aggregate data, and statistics. Not that these indirect approaches are wrong or useless. They have their own value, and there may be a loss of perspective (the big picture) when one relies solely on direct observation. But direct observation is essential, and no combination of indirect methods, however clever, can possibly take its place.

Dallis's previous experience managing plants might have prepared him to look at operations of greater scale and scope, but had Takahashi given him a project with greater scope, Dallis might not have learned to observe with such precision. Dallis's first six weeks at the U.S. engine plant meant that he had up to

23,824 opportunities to observe complete work cycles. Because his work was limited to a 19-person line, he could view more than a thousand work cycles per person. That gave him deep insight into the line's productivity and safety.

LESSON 2

PROPOSED CHANGES SHOULD ALWAYS BE STRUCTURED AS EXPERIMENTS.

In the scientific method, experiments are used to test a hypothesis, and the results are used to refine or reject the hypothesis. Dallis's problem solving was structured so that he embedded explicit and testable assumptions in his analysis of the work. Throughout his training, therefore, he had to explain gaps between predicted and actual results. In his meetings with Takahashi at the U.S. engine plant, for example, he was required to propose hypotheses on Monday and the results of his experiments on Friday. In Japan, he had to present his changes as tests of causal relationships, stating the problem he saw, the root cause he suspected, the change he had made, and the countermeasure's actual effect on performance.

Of course, many people trying to improve a process have some idea of what the problems are and how to fix them. The difference with TPS—and this is key—is that it seeks to fully understand both the problem and the solution. For example, any manager might say, "Maybe the parts rack should be closer to the assembler's hand. If we move it here, I'll bet it'll shave a few seconds off the cycle." Were he to try this and find that it saved six seconds, he would probably be quite pleased and consider the problem solved.

But in the eyes of a Toyota manager like Takahashi, such a result would indicate that the manager didn't fully understand the work that he was trying to improve. Why hadn't he been more specific about how far he was going to move the rack? And how many seconds did he *expect* to save? Four? If the actual savings is six seconds, that's cause for celebration—but also for additional inquiry. Why was there a two-second difference? With the explicit precision encouraged by Takahashi, the discrepancy would prompt a deeper investigation into how a process worked and, perhaps more important, how a particular person studied and improved the process.

LESSON 3

WORKERS AND MANAGERS SHOULD EXPERIMENT AS FREQUENTLY AS POSSIBLE.

At Toyota, the focus is on many quick, simple experiments rather than on a few lengthy, complex ones. This became particularly evident when Dallis went to Japan. Whereas in the United States he made 25 changes in six weeks (before the weekend blitz during which 75 were completed), in Japan he had to make 50 changes in 2≡ shifts, which meant an average of one change every 22 minutes. This encouraged Dallis to learn from making small incremental changes rather than large system-design changes. He would observe work actually being done, quickly see where struggles were occurring, then rapidly test his understanding by implementing a countermeasure, thereby accelerating the rate at which he discovered "contingencies" or "interferences" in the process. This is precisely the way Toyota workers practice process improvement. They cannot "practice" making a change, because a change can be made only once. But they can practice the process of observing and testing many times.

To ensure that Dallis received the practice he needed and that he internalized his understanding of it, Takahashi structured Dallis's training so that the complexity of his experiments increased gradually. When Dallis started at the U.S. engine plant, he conducted "single factor" experiments, changing small, individual work elements rather than taking a system perspective. What's more, his efforts there started with individual work methods, progressing to more complex and subtle machine problems only when he had developed his observation and problem-solving skills over the six weeks. Thus, he moved from problems that were easier to observe to those that were harder. If each learning cycle is kept small and bounded, then the learner can make mistakes and the consequences will not be severe. This approach increases the learner's willingness to take risks and learn by doing. Dallis's training at Kamigo mirrored this progression: He began, once again, with work-method issues of "overburden" before moving on to machines.[2]

LESSON 4

MANAGERS SHOULD COACH, NOT FIX.

Dallis's training not only gave him insight into how Toyota delivers continuous improvement but also helped him understand the unique relationships between Toyota's managers and workers. Dallis himself had been rewarded by his previous employer for being a problem solver, albeit one with a more participative and inclusive approach than most. What he saw at Toyota, by contrast, was workers and low-level managers constantly solving problems. Indeed, the more senior the manager, the less likely he was to be solving problems himself.

Toyota managers act as enablers. Throughout Dallis's training, Takahashi—one of Toyota's most senior operational managers—positioned himself as a teacher and coach, not as a technological specialist. He put Dallis through experiences without explicitly stating what or how he was to learn. Even when specific skills were imparted, these were purely to assist Dallis's observation and experimentation. For instance, Takahashi showed Dallis how to observe an individual worker in order to spot instances of stress, wasted effort, and so on, and he explicitly advised Dallis on how to develop prototypes. But at no point did he suggest actual process improvements. Rather, he directed Dallis on how to find opportunities for those improvements (as in, study this person or that machine, looking for various types of stress, strain, or faults) and on how to develop and test possible countermeasures.

Takahashi also gave Dallis the resources he needed to act quickly. For example, at Kamigo, Dallis had the help of a maintenance worker to move equipment, create fixtures, relocate wires and pipes, and provide other skilled trade work so that he could test as many ideas as possible. Takahashi and the shop manager also came to the cell of the machining operation to review Dallis's ideas; they gave him tips on piloting his changes before asking support workers to make parts or relocate equipment. When Dallis wanted to rotate some gauges that tested parts, the shop manager showed him how to quickly and inexpensively make cardboard prototypes to test location, orientation, size, and so on.

The result of this unusual manager–worker relationship is a high degree of sophisticated problem solving at all levels of the organization. Dallis noted, "As a former engine-plant person, I saw a line [at Kamigo] that was 15 years old but that had the capacity to build 90 different engine types. It was amazing that they solved so many problems with such simple equipment. Behind the changes was some pretty deep thinking." The basic company philosophy is that any operating system can be improved if enough people at every level are looking and experimenting closely enough. (After all, if only the big shots were expected to make changes, all that "little" stuff would get overlooked.) The fact that Dallis, after just three months at the U.S. engine plant, was able to empower others to implement 50 improvements at Kamigo, one of Toyota's top plants, offers insight into why Toyota stays ahead of its competitors.[3]

Back to America

To see if Dallis had learned the right lessons from his training, Takahashi sent him back to the U.S. engine plant where his instruction had begun. As we have seen, Dallis had already helped make substantial improvements in the assembly line's labor productivity and ergonomic safety before going to Japan. But he hadn't been able to raise operational availability to 95%. Now, upon Dallis's return to that plant, Takahashi had him attempt this goal again. However, there was a marked departure from Dallis's earlier approach, in which he primarily saw himself as a problem solver.

With Takahashi's help, Dallis worked with the line's group leader and assistant manager in order to develop the problem-solving skills of the line's team members and team leaders. The point was for the team to learn to solve little problems simultaneously so that the line could recover quickly when problems occurred. For instance, the team realized that it had difficulties in keeping track of what work needed to be done and in identifying problems as they occurred. It therefore had to improve its "visual management" of the work—what was going well, what was going wrong, and what needed to be done. Dallis sat down with the group leader and assistant manager and set out a schedule for identifying specific problems and allocating responsibility for them across the team. As the team members observed and developed countermeasures, Dallis would drop by much as Takahashi had done, asking them specific questions that would oblige them to observe their allotted problems more closely as they happened. To its delight, the group hit its mark ahead of schedule and raised operational availability to 99%.

Dallis had returned to America with an altered focus. He had realized from the way Takahashi had managed his training, and from what he'd seen of others' training, that the efforts of a senior manager like himself should be aimed not at making direct improvements but at producing a cadre of excellent group leaders who learn through continuous experimentation. The target of 95% operational availability at the U.S. engine plant was the same, but he now knew whose target it really was, and it wasn't his. At this point, Takahashi finally released Dallis from his training to take on his full-time managerial responsibilities.

F OR ANYONE TRYING to understand how the Toyota Production System really works, there is probably no substitute for the kind of total immersion that Dallis received. TPS is a system you have to live to fully understand, let alone improve. Besides, anyone like Dallis coming into Toyota from the outside, regardless of his or her experience, is coming into an organization with a long history of making improvements and modifications at a pace few organizations have ever approached. No one can expect to assimilate—let alone recreate—such a strong and distinct culture in just a few weeks or even a few months. Nevertheless, any company that develops and implements a training program such as the one Dallis participated in is sure to reap enormous dividends. The organization that applies the rules in designing its operations and that trains its managers to apply those rules will have made a good start at replicating the DNA of the Toyota Production System.

The Power of Principles

THE INSIGHT THAT TOYOTA APPLIES underlying principles rather than specific tools and processes explains why the company continues to outperform its competitors. Many companies have tried to imitate Toyota's tools as opposed to its principles; as a result, many have ended up with rigid, inflexible production systems that worked well in the short term but didn't stand the test of time.

Recognizing that TPS is about applying principles rather than tools enables companies that in no way resemble Toyota to tap into its sources of success. Alcoa, a company whose large-scale processes—refining, smelting, and so on—bear little resemblance to Toyota's discrete-parts fabrication and assembly operations, has based its Alcoa Business System (ABS) on the TPS rules. Alcoa claims that ABS saved the company $1.1 billion from 1998 to 2000, while improving safety, productivity, and quality.

In another example, pilot projects applying the rules at the University of Pittsburgh Medical Center and other health care organizations have led to huge improvements in medication administration, nursing, and other critical processes, delivering better quality care to patients, relieving workers of nonproductive burdens, as well as providing costs savings and operating efficiencies.

Notes

1. Operational availability equals machine run time/ machine use time. For instance, if a machine requires eight minutes of process time to grind a surface, but, because of jams and other interruptions, ten minutes are actually spent from start to finish, then operational availability would be 80%. Ideally, operationally availability would be 100%—that is, the machine always runs when it is needed.

2. The incremental approach was also helpful to Takahashi, who used it to teach Dallis. He directly observed Dallis's work by creating short learning cycles with rapid feedback so that he could continually reassess Dallis's knowledge and skills, both to provide feedback in order to help him learn and to design the next learning increment.

3. According to Takahashi, the expectation was that group leaders at Kamigo—managers who supervised several operating shops or cells—would spend 70% of their time doing process improvement work. This time would often

be shared among three to four teams, implying that team leaders—people managing one shop or cell—were expected to spend a minimum of 20% of their time on improvement work.

Originally published in May 2004
Reprint R0405E

Another Look at How Toyota Integrates Product Development

DURWARD K. SOBEK II, JEFFREY K. LIKER,
AND ALLEN C. WARD

Executive Summary

CHALLENGED BY WORLD-CLASS COMPETITORS, manufacturing companies in the United States have greatly improved their product development efforts as well as their factory operations. Today, however, U.S. companies are beginning to see the effectiveness of their product development systems plateau. More important, that effectiveness seems to have leveled off far short of the best Japanese companies.

The authors explore how one of those companies, Toyota, manages its vehicle development process. Toyota's managerial practices can be grouped into six organizational mechanisms. Three of them are primarily social processes: mutual adjustment, mentoring supervision, and integrative leadership from product heads. The other three are forms of standardization: standard skills, standard work processes, and design standards. Alone, each mechanism would accomplish little, but every piece has its own role and at the same time reinforces the others, unlike many of the sophisticated tools and practices at U.S. companies that tend to be implemented independently.

Together, the mechanisms give Toyota a tightly linked product-development system that relies on training and standardization to achieve cross-functional coordination while still building functional expertise. Toyota has added a number of *twists* to ensure that each project has the flexibility it needs and still benefits from what other projects have learned. This balance allows Toyota to achieve integration across projects and over time, as well as within projects.

CHALLENGED BY WORLD-CLASS competitors, manufacturing companies in the United States have undergone a renaissance in the last decade. The renaissance started on the shop floor with an emphasis on built-in quality, the elimination of waste, and faster throughputs. But attention quickly turned upstream to product development, where Japanese companies were outperforming U.S. competitors on nearly every measure: speed to market, design quality, product-design manufacturability, cost, and productivity. Observers concluded that the key to Japanese success, and U.S. industry's weakness, was integration—both between product design and manufacturing-process design, and with marketing, purchasing, finance, and other business functions.

A great many companies attacked the issue head on. Typical solutions were such product-development tools as quality function deployment and Taguchi methods. Companies also introduced organizational solutions; those solutions ranged from keeping the basic functional organization intact and assigning people to temporary project teams to disbanding the functional organization altogether in favor of organizing around products, as Chrysler did in the early 1990s. (Here we use the term *function* broadly to mean the various groups of specialized expertise required to make new models work—including the engineering specialties within the design process, such as electrical, body, or test engineering, as well as other business functions, such as manufacturing and marketing.)

The new solutions have brought substantial improvements to the companies and dramatic results in the marketplace. But they have also created problems of their own. Cross-functional coordination has improved, but at the cost of depth of knowledge within functions, because people are spending less time within their functions. Organizational learning across projects has also dropped as people rotate rapidly through positions. Standardization across products has suffered because product teams have become autonomous. In organizations that combine functional and project-based structures, engineers are often torn between the orders of their functional bosses on the one hand and the demands of project leaders on the other. As these new problems take their toll, U.S. companies are beginning to see the effectiveness of their product-development systems plateau. More important, that effectiveness seems to have leveled off far short of the best Japanese companies.

This article explores how one of those companies, Toyota, manages its vehicle-development process. We studied Toyota's process for five years through in-depth interviews at all levels of management. Interestingly, we found that in many ways the company does not resemble what is often considered the model of Japanese product development—it has maintained a functionally based organization while achieving its impressive degree of integration, and many of its practices are actually similar to those that U.S. companies employed during their manufacturing prime earlier in this century.

We can group Toyota's managerial practices into six organizational mechanisms. Three of them are primarily social processes: mutual adjustment, close supervision, and integrative leadership from product heads. The other three are forms of standardization: standard skills, standard work processes, and design standards. Alone, each mechanism would accomplish little, but every piece has its own role and at the same time reinforces the others, unlike many of the sophisticated tools and practices at companies in the United States, which tend to be implemented independently.

Together, the mechanisms give Toyota a tightly linked product-development system that achieves cross-functional coordination while still building functional expertise. This balance allows the company to achieve integration across projects and over time, as well as within projects. U.S. companies have concentrated on bringing the functions together within projects, but a single-minded focus on that goal can actually undermine attempts to share information across projects. Cross-functional teams, for example, work well within individual projects, but the temporary, personal nature of these teams makes it hard for them to transmit information to teams on other projects.

Toyota, by contrast, seems to go to the opposite organizational extreme. It relies on highly formalized rules and standards, and puts limits on the use of cross-functional teams. Such rigid policies can have enormous drawbacks. To avoid those drawbacks, Toyota has added a number of *twists* to ensure that each project has the flexibility it needs and still benefits from what other projects have learned. The result is a deftly managed process that rivals the company's famous production system, lean manufacturing, in effectiveness.

Coordination Based on Writing

One of the most powerful ways to coordinate one's efforts with those of people in other functions is to talk to them face to face. In this manner, each party gets the other's point of view and can quickly make adjustments to find common ground. This *mutual adjustment* often takes the form of a meeting: a product designer and a manufacturing engineer, for example, get together to discuss the effects that a proposed design for a particular car body would have on the cost of production.

Direct contact between the members of different functions is certainly important—some say it is the essential ingredient in getting functional groups that have traditionally been at odds to work together. Indeed, many observers, managers, and engineers claim that face-to-face interaction is the richest, most appropriate form of communication for product development. Numerous companies now colocate functional experts so that interaction can occur with much greater ease and frequency. Often these companies have done away with written forms of communication because, as some claim, written reports and memos do not have the richness of information or interactive qualities needed for product development.

Meetings, however, are costly in terms of time and efficiency, and meeting time increases with colocation. Meetings usually involve limited value-added work per person, and they easily lose focus and drag on longer than necessary. Engineers in companies we've visited often complain of not having enough time to get their engineering work done because of all the meetings in their schedule.

Toyota, by contrast, does not colocate engineers or assign them to dedicated project teams. Most people reside within functional areas and are simply assigned to work on projects—often more than one at a time—led by project leaders. By rooting engineers in a function, the company ensures that the functions develop deep specialized knowledge and experience.

In lieu of regularly scheduled meetings, the company emphasizes written communication. When an issue surfaces that requires cross-functional coordination, the protocol is first to write a report that presents the diagnosis of the problem, key information, and recommendations, and then to distribute this document to the concerned parties. Usually, the report is accompanied by either a phone call or a short meeting to highlight the key points and emphasize the importance of the information. The recipient is expected to read and study the document and to offer feedback, sometimes in the form of a separate written report. One or two iterations communicate a great deal of information, and participants typically arrive at an agreement on most, if not all, items. If there are outstanding disagreements, then it's time to hold a meeting to hammer out a decision face to face.

In such problem-solving meetings, participants already understand the key issues, are all working from a common set of data, and have thought about and prepared proposals and responses. The meeting can focus on solving the specific problem without wasting time bringing people up to speed. By contrast, at many U.S. companies, attendees often arrive at meetings having done little or no preparation. They can spend the first half of the meeting just defining the issue, and responses are shoot-from-the-hip reactions to a problem that people have had little time to think about.

Toyota takes its focused style of meeting quite seriously. One engineer we talked to showed us his schedule for the day, which included two meetings at separate times with the same group of people. When asked why he would schedule separate meetings with this group, he explained that they needed two meetings to discuss two distinct problems. It was important not to confuse the issues by combining them into one meeting.

Once the writer of the original report has consulted with all interested parties, he or she writes a final version of the report that presents all sides of the question. The overall reporting process therefore has two benefits. First, it documents and summarizes analysis and decision making in a convenient form for the rest of the organization. Second, and more important, it forces engineers in every function to gather opinions from other functions regarding the ramifications of the changes they are proposing.

Twist: Although Toyota often relies on written communication as the first line of attack in solving problems, it does not suffer from the voluminous paperwork we associate with bureaucracy. In most cases, engineers write short, crisp reports on one side of size A3 paper (roughly 11 × 17, the largest faxable size). The reports all follow the same format so that everyone knows where to find the definition of the problem, the responsible engineer and department, the results of the analysis, and the recommendations. The standard format also helps engineers make sure they have covered the important angles. The result is a clear statement of a problem and solutions that is accessible not only to people within a particular project but also to those working on other projects.

Writing these reports is a difficult but useful skill, so the company gives its engineers formal training in how to boil down what they want to communicate. Supervisors see to it that engineers do the appropriate groundwork to ensure that all pertinent views are taken into consideration. Toyota has also created a culture in which reading these reports is highly valued and essential to doing one's job well. Indeed, we heard about a certain Toyota executive who refused to read any report longer than two pages.

Mentoring Supervisors

In product development, supervision traditionally took place within individual functions. Electrical engineers, for example, were supervised by other electrical engineers because only they fully understood the work involved. Recently, some U.S. companies have experimented with cross-functional team-based organizations in order to force engineers to think beyond the needs of their own function. Chrysler, for example, is organized around product platforms rather than functions, and the platform team leader heads all product engineering in the platform.

Toyota, however, has not forgotten the value of instructive supervision within functions. Supervisors and higher-level managers are deeply involved in the details of engineering design. In fact, young engineers (anyone with less than ten years' experience) must usually get approval from their functional supervisors not only for the designs they propose but also for each step involved in the process of arriving at the final design.

The company depends on supervisors to build deep functional expertise in its new hires—expertise that then facilitates coordination across functions. But functional supervisors also teach engineers how to write reports, whom to send the reports to, how to interpret reports from other functions, and how to prepare for meetings. Direct supervision thus works in concert with mutual adjustment in order to promote coordination.

Twist: To American eyes, such intensive supervision would seem to be a kind of meddling that stifles the creativity and learning of new engineers and other specialists. U.S. companies are moving in the opposite direction as they preach empowerment, with superiors acting as facilitators rather than bosses. But Toyota has succeeded in keeping its supervision fresh and engaging, in two ways. Like Toyota's supervisors on the factory floor, managers in product development are working engineers. Instead of merely managing the engineering process, they hone their engineering skills, stay abreast of new technology, maintain their contacts and develop new ones, and remain involved in the creative process itself. Functional engineers are not frustrated by the experience of working under someone less skilled than they are. In many U.S. companies, by contrast, engineers who rise through the ranks become managers who stop doing engineering work.

Perhaps more important, Toyota's managers seem to avoid making decisions for their subordinates. They rarely tell subordinates what to do and instead answer questions with questions. They force engineers to think about and understand the problem before pursuing an alternative, even if the managers already know the correct answer. It's not a boss-subordinate or even a coach-athlete relationship, but a student-mentor relationship.

Integrative Leaders

Perhaps the most powerful way to integrate the work of people from diverse specialties is to have a leader with a broad overview of the whole. Many U.S. companies have recently been moving toward a *heavyweight-project-management* structure. Heavyweight project managers coordinate all the specialists from functional departments around a common project with a common set of goals. Their authority in these matrix organizations comes from their complete control over their particular project rather than from any direct supervisory authority over the individual functions.

Toyota's equivalent is the *chief engineer.* Each chief engineer, based in one of Toyota's three vehicle-development centers (which oversee long-term planning across projects), maintains full responsibility for a single vehicle program but wields no direct power over the functions.

Indeed, Toyota's chief engineers come close to matching what others have described as the prototypical heavyweight project manager. Before attaining their position, they must demonstrate both exemplary technical expertise and fluency in synthesizing technical knowledge into clever, innovative designs. Toyota's managers feel strongly that only a good designer can evaluate the quality of someone else's design. Chief engineers also need to be able to conceptualize whole systems. It is one thing to understand the mechanics of a brake system and another to apply that knowledge toward an actual brake system design; but it is quite another thing to be able to conceptualize a brake system and visualize how it can be integrated with the rest of the vehicle. By contrast, a number of companies with heavyweight product managers do not have such stringent technical requirements.

All chief engineers have a small staff of 5 to 15 engineers to assist them in managing the development process and in coordinating the work of the functional specialties. The hundreds of other engineers on the project report only through the functional chain of command. The chief engineer has no formal authority over them, so he must "persuade" them to help him realize his vision for the vehicle. One former chief engineer described the position as being the "president of the vehicle": just as the U.S. president heads the country but has no direct authority over legislation (beyond vetoes), so a chief engineer cannot dictate what functional engineers do. But his extensive technical expertise wins him tremendous respect, even admiration, from functional engineers—a key source of his enormous informal authority.

The limits on the chief engineers' power, despite their prestige, are real, and the engineering expertise and equal rank of the general managers in charge of the functional areas can keep chief engineers from making potentially dangerous mistakes. For example, in designing a new model of the Celica sports car several years ago, the styling department suggested a longer front-quarter panel. The change would have increased the panel's extension into the top of the front door, allowing the door to curve back at the top, thereby creating an angular and more exciting look. The manufacturing engineer assigned to door panels, however, opposed the change because the altered panel would be difficult to produce.

After assessing both sides, the chief engineer for the vehicle favored the altered front panel. Nevertheless, the manufacturing engineer felt strongly that the change was unwise. If Toyota had organized around projects rather than functions, styling would likely have gotten its way, and the car might well have suffered production problems. But because the chief engineer's authority was only informal, the manufacturing engineer was able to raise the issue to the level of the general manager of manufacturing, who strongly challenged the chief engineer. After substantial argument, the two sides reached an innovative compromise that achieved the cutaway look that styling wanted with a satisfactory level of manufacturability.

Such incidents explain why one Toyota engineer, when asked what makes a good car, replied, "Lots of conflict." Conflict occurs when people from different functional areas clearly represent the issues from their perspective. Its absence implies that some functional areas are being too accommodating—to the detriment of the project as a whole. Still, when managers resolve conflicts through organizational influence, horse trading, or executive fiat, the results are often poor. It is the ability of chief engineers to see the broad picture clearly—and the ability of functional managers to contain the chief engineer's enthusiasm—that leads to highly integrated designs. And while the chief engineers keep individual projects on track, the autonomous functional engineers and managers ensure that knowledge and experience from other projects are not forgotten in the current one.

Twist: Chief engineers do differ in one important respect from even the best heavyweight project managers. The latter typically delegate decision making to functional teams, while retaining authority over the team's decisions and taking responsibility for implementing those decisions throughout the development process. If a heavyweight project manager doesn't like a decision, he or she can veto it. By contrast, a chief engineer takes the initiative by personally making key vehiclewide decisions. His authority over design decisions stems from the fact that the vehicle is quite clearly "his car." He is therefore less the manager of and more the lead designer on the overall project.

As lead designer, chief engineers design (and subsequently manage) the entire process of developing the product, and they personally articulate the vehicle concept that becomes the blueprint for the entire program. That concept includes the major dimensions of the vehicle; decisions on such major systems as the transmission; the variety of models to be offered; the characteristics of the target customer; sales projections; and targets on weight, cost, and fuel economy. Chief engineers integrate the work of the functions by planning how all the parts will work together as a cohesive whole, soliciting input from the various engineering, manufacturing, and marketing functions, of course. Once a chief engineer has designed the overall approach for a car, the different functions fill in the technical details that are required to realize the vehicle concept.

Some of the remaining integration problems at U.S. companies may in fact stem from a lack of precisely this kind of system design. Even companies with able heavyweight product managers tend to jump directly from product concept to the technical details of engineering design. They bypass, without going through, the very difficult but important task of designing the overall vehicle system: planning how all the parts will work together as a cohesive whole before sweating the fine details. At Toyota, the chief engineer provides the glue that binds the whole process together.

Standard Skills

Every company depends on highly skilled engineers, designers, and technicians to bring a product to market. Organizations can coordinate their activities by giving each person within a specialty the same set of skills to accomplish his or her tasks. When we know what to expect of others because they are trained in a certain way, we can request specific services with relatively little effort in coordination. In engineering, most U.S. companies rely heavily on universities or specialized training companies to provide their people with the skills needed to do their jobs.

Toyota, by contrast, relies primarily on training within the company. It views training as a key competency, worth developing internally rather than outsourcing. Engineers receive most of their training through the intensive mentoring involved in direct supervision, although the company also runs a training center with instructors who are experienced Toyota engineers. The process not only develops excellent engineers but also teaches new hires Toyota's distinct approach to developing the body, chassis, or other systems in a vehicle.

Additionally, Toyota rotates most of its engineers within only one function, unlike U.S. companies, which tend to rotate their people among functions. Body engineers, for example, will work on different auto-body subsystems (for example, door hardware or outer panels) for most, if not all, of their careers. Because most engineers rotate primarily within their engineering function, they gain the experience that encourages standard work, making the outputs of each functional group predictable to other functions. In addition, rotations generally occur at longer intervals than the typical product cycle so that engineers can see and learn from the results of their work.

That consistency over time means that the company's engineers in the manufacturing division, for example, need to spend less time and energy communicating and coordinating with their counterparts in design because they learn what to expect from them. Indeed, Toyota firmly believes that deep expertise in engineering specialties is essential to its product-development system. We often heard such comments as, "It takes ten years to make a body engineer" in our conversations with the company's managers. In short, the widely held notion that Japanese companies rotate their personnel broadly and frequently simply does not apply to Toyota.

Twist #1: Rotating locally and building functional expertise would seem to create rigid functional boundaries, or *chimneys,* in which engineers work only to be the best in their function. An electrical engineer, for example, might aim to develop the most elaborate electrical design possible, without thinking about how that design will work with the rest of the vehicle. But we have found that the so-called chimney effect is not the result of young engineers being too loyal to their functions or too narrow-minded about what cars need. Rather, it is usually the result of experienced engineers and managers hoarding their knowledge, which becomes the basis of their power in an organization rooted in functions.

To avoid such political conflict, Toyota takes care to rotate most of its senior people broadly. Engineers at the *bucho* level—which usually means the head of a functional division (for example, power-train engineering for front-wheel-drive passenger cars) with at least 20 years' experience—typically rotate widely across the company to areas outside their expertise. Such moves force buchos to rely heavily on the experts in their new area, building broad networks of mutual obligation. At the same time, buchos bring their own experience, expertise, and network of contacts that they can use to facilitate integration.

Twist #2: Buchos (and chief engineers) encourage their people to see the needs of the product as a whole, but Toyota also keeps design engineers aware of the ramifications of their decisions throughout the development process. These engineers retain responsibility for their parts of the car from the concept stage to the start of full production. A door-systems engineer, for example, works with stylists to determine the concept of the door and then develops the detailed design by working with production engineers and outside suppliers. The engineer also goes to the factory to be part of the launch team as the vehicle ramps up to full production.

Flexible Work Standards

The stereotypical bureaucratic way of coordinating work processes is to specify in detail the content of each step in the process. Tasks are preprogrammed so that one group knows what to expect from another and when to expect it, with little or no communication required. Factories use this kind of coordination extensively, standardizing the tasks at each workstation to ensure that the work is done consistently and in a set amount of time. All the workstations can then be easily coordinated by a schedule.

Many U.S. companies have tried to apply this concept to product development, notably General Motors with its *four-phase process.* A special team at GM defines the process in great detail, telling each department what it needs to do when, whom to send results to, what format the information should take, and so on. The plan for the styling function alone covers the length of one wall in a sizable conference room. The four-phase process is almost never followed as its authors envisioned, however, because the process is so detailed that every vehicle pro- gram has exceptions that force designers to deviate from the prescribed process—the real world resists such inten- sive planning. In addition, a separate group develops and maintains the details of the standard process; as a result, the people who must follow the process do not have own- ership of it, and the prescribed processes are not likely to be truly representative of the actual one. Indeed, the four- phase process seems to do little to shorten cycle times or to bring other benefits that such thorough planning aims to produce. Companies such as General Motors face a dilemma: the more they attempt to define the process of product development, the less the organization is able to carry out that process properly.

Toyota, by contrast, has successfully standardized much of its development process. Product-engineering departments follow highly consistent processes for developing subsystems within a vehicle. Routine work procedures—such as design blueprints, A3 reports, and feedback forms for design reviews—are also highly stan- dardized. The overall process of developing a vehicle fol- lows regular milestones. Indeed, the suppliers we visited in Japan could describe from memory Toyota's vehicle-development process because it is so consistent from model to model. Every model has a concept, styling approval, one or two prototype vehicles, two trial production runs, and finally a launch; and suppliers know the approximate timing of each event. (For more on how Toyota uses standards to coordinate its work with suppliers, see "A Second Look at Japanese Product Development," by Rajan R. Kamath and Jeffrey K. Liker, HBR November–December 1994.)

Twist #1: How does Toyota avoid the pitfalls that other companies have experienced with work standards? When you talk specifics with Toyota engineers—such as how many prototypes are built and tested, when designs are finalized, or how long a particular phase takes—the response is typically that it varies case by case. The actual standardized work plans are kept to a minimum; they often fit on a single sheet of paper. The basic process in the eyes of the participants is very consistent from model to model, but the implementation of the concept is individually designed for each vehicle program. Intense socialization of engineers through on-the-job training creates a deep understanding of every step, as well as a broad understanding of the expectations at milestones and final deadlines. The simplified plans allow flexibility, common understanding, and continuous improvement, while hard deadlines keep the project on track. The company thus gains the efficiencies offered by standards without stifling its engineers. The standards also save product developers the trouble of reinventing a new process for each individual project.

Twist #2: Another difference is that the standard work procedures are maintained by the people and departments that use them, not by a centralized staff that may be tempted to standardize for the sake of standardization. As a result, standards are more likely to be simple and to the point, relevant and up-to-date. They are therefore more likely to be followed. In addition, the people who use the standards understand their intent, so deviations are perfectly permissible as long as consistency (and thus predictability for other functions) is maintained. At Toyota, developing the product and designing standard development processes are considered to be inseparable tasks.

Living Design Standards

In the past, product developers often used standardized product rules to guide their work. Many companies, however, seem to have shied away from design standards in recent years. Engineers at automakers in the United States have told us time and again that design standards are largely ignored at their companies. Arguing that technology is changing too fast for standards to be valuable, they boast about "starting from a clean sheet of paper" in new product-development projects. (Test engineers, of course, rely on standards to ensure that the final product meets government regulations and other requirements, but those guidelines concern the product's function instead of providing information for the product's design.) Design standards appear to be archaic or stifling to companies that depend on innovation for success.

Toyota, however, still maintains voluminous books of engineering checklists to guide design work. These checklists act as the first cut at designing manufacturable products that use common parts across platforms.

Engineering checklists contain detailed information concerning any number of aspects, including functionality, manufacturability, government regulations, and reliability. The styling department, for example, has a checklist for the license-plate well that contains plate dimensions, bolt hole locations, regulations on tilt angles and illumination for various world markets, and restrictions on curvature radii. And every part of the car body has a separate manufacturing checklist that shows what angles will produce a good part, what kinds of interfaces avoid problems in assembly, and other guidelines.

Engineers use the checklists to guide the design throughout the development process. The checklists are particularly important for the intensive design reviews that every vehicle program undergoes. Hundreds of engineers come together to study a vehicle or prototype at key junctures, looking for problems and opportunities for improvement. What keeps these extremely large meetings from becoming chaotic is that all engineers come with a list of all the items they need to verify from their perspective. If the design conforms to the checklist, the part is highly likely to meet a certain level of functionality, manufacturability, quality, and reliability. If it does not, discrepancies between the checklists and the design become the focal points of discussion among the divisions. The design review checklists are another example of using written forms of communication to improve face-to-face meetings.

Once in place, design standards add predictability across vehicle subsystems, and between product design engineers and manufacturing engineers. The engineer responsible for audio speakers, for example, can take advantage of existing specifications for door sizes and door components and can begin designing speakers without coordinating directly with the other engineers working on door components. As a result, Toyota is able to bring new products to market quickly—as it demonstrated with the RAV4 mini-sport-utility vehicle, which was brought to market in 24 months, carved out a new product niche in Japan, but still drew on existing design standards for 80% of its makeup.

Engineering checklists also facilitate organizational learning across generations of vehicles. Toyota trains its engineers not only to record product histories but also to abstract from that experience in order to update existing capabilities. When an engineer learns something new, the knowledge can be incorporated into the checklist and then applied across the company to every subsequent vehicle. Those lessons reside with the organization, not in one person's head. If an engineer leaves, the knowledge he or she has gained is captured in the checklists and remains with the company. Just as standardization is the key to continuous improvement on the factory floor, standards are the basis for continuous improvement in engineering design.

Twist #1: Again, such standardization smacks of the kind of bureaucratic approach that U.S. companies seem bent on avoiding. But rather than presenting design rules that have been imposed by a central staff, the checklists explicitly define current capabilities as understood by the responsible designers. They are living documents: product and manufacturing engineers update the standards with every vehicle program. New information is quickly and efficiently disseminated throughout the organization and into interfacing divisions, without any meetings taking place.

Twist #2: Toyota's continuous and overlapping product cycles also help keep standards fresh. The company launches new vehicles on a regular basis, several times every year. It also has annual product renewals, and a major model change every three to four years, unlike other companies that stretch out their product cycles. Accordingly, standards are revisited every couple of months (as opposed to being used once and then put away for a couple of years); they never become outdated. The frequent changes to the checklists also give engineers continual opportunities to develop and hone their skills.

Managing Product Development as a System

Together, these six mechanisms make up a whole system, each part supporting the others. Mentoring supervision serves mainly to build functional expertise, but it also teaches young engineers how to write and interpret reports, work with chief engineers, and understand and use standards. The chief engineer's prestige reinforces the importance of expertise while it also balances out the functional bent of the other engineers. The chief engineer also promotes mutual adjustment by providing the working instructions for each vehicle program and by resolving cross-functional disagreements.

For their part, the three types of standards interact and support one another to boost the pace of development; at the same time, they allow flexibility and build Toyota's base of knowledge. Without the other mechanisms providing reinforcement, each mechanism would not be nearly as effective. (See the exhibit "How the Coordinating Mechanisms Work Together.")

Indeed, the two halves of Toyota's system—social processes and standards—interact in powerful ways. The functional organization, with its intensive mentoring, trains and socializes engineers in ways that foster in-depth technical knowledge and efficient communication. Without deep tacit knowledge about how to develop products, standardization would become a bureaucratic nightmare. In turn, the common use of the different standards makes all functions automatically aware of the constraints imposed by interfacing groups and gives focus to reports and meetings. Toyota shows that companies do not need to choose between functional depth and cross-functional coordination—each can facilitate the other within the right environment.

Toyota's balanced approach also benefits from basic company policies that provide a foundation for the whole system. With a stable and long-term workforce, the company can afford to invest heavily in training and socializing its engineers; it knows that the investment will pay off for many years. The company also places great emphasis on satisfying customers. Most of its engineers in Japan, for example, are required to sell cars door to door for a few weeks in their first year of hire. Both factors help discourage the functional loyalties that might otherwise afflict a company with Toyota's structure.

These synergistic interactions give Toyota's system its stability and power. They enable the automaker to integrate across projects as well as within them. Design standards, for example, facilitate integration across functions while promoting the use of common components in simultaneous projects, and provide a ready base of knowledge for the next generation of products.

How the Coordinating Mechanisms Work Together

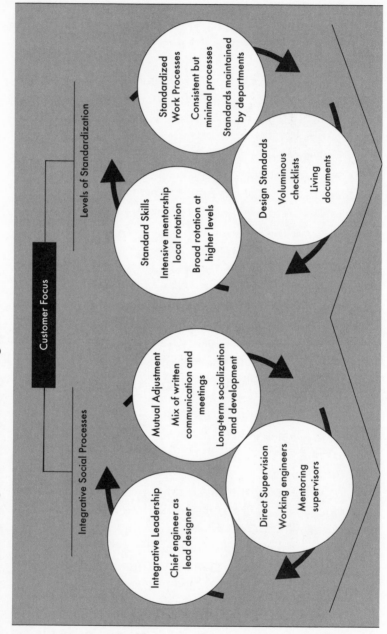

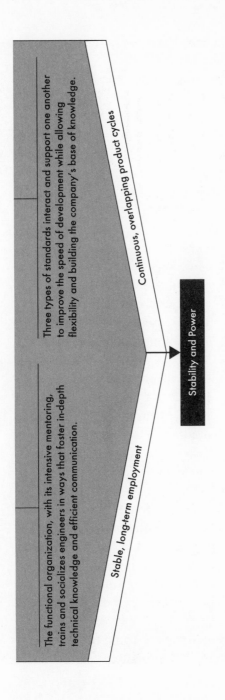

The functional organization, with its intensive mentoring, trains and socializes engineers in ways that foster in-depth technical knowledge and efficient communication.

Three types of standards interact and support one another to improve the speed of development while allowing flexibility and building the company's base of knowledge.

Stable, long-term employment

Continuous, overlapping product cycles

Stability and Power

Implications for Other Companies

Toyota's mix of practices may not be right for other
industries, or even for other companies in the auto
industry. Different environments, different corporate
cultures, and different circumstances mean that a company's product-development system must be uniquely
designed to suit its distinct needs. Indeed, Toyota's system is not necessarily perfect even for Toyota. Although
the company has succeeded mightily with its new products in mass-market sedans and luxury cars—two well-
defined segments of the marketplace—it has reacted late
to the recent major shifts in consumer demand: first to
minivans and then to sport-utility vehicles. So design
standards and internal socialization, for example, may
make for nimble and innovative product development,
but perhaps at the cost of discouraging some big leaps
in thinking.

Nevertheless, we believe that Toyota's system has
important implications for other companies. First,
integrated product-development processes should be
developed and implemented as coherent systems. Individual best practices and tools are helpful, but their
potential can be fully realized only if they are integrated into and reinforce the overall system. Toyota
was fortunate in that it was able to develop its system
over decades through an incremental, almost uncon-
scious, process of taking good ideas and adapting them
to the existing structure. Other companies that conclude they are going down the wrong track and need a
major overhaul of their product-development systems
do not have the luxury of developing their system
gradually over time. They will need to be much more
conscious of designing a coherent system.

Second, well-designed systems should balance the demands of functional expertise and cross-functional coordination. The chart "How Toyota Avoids Extremes" describes features of the two opposing sides: the *chimney extreme*, characterized by strong functional divisions, and the *committee extreme*, characterized by broad-based decision making and weak functional expertise. Toyota, for example, uses both written forms of communication and face-to-face contact to the extent that each is useful and efficient.

Achieving the proper balance, however, is no easy task. Many of Toyota's current practices—such as an emphasis on written communication, design standards, and the chief engineer—seem to have been standard practice in the United States in the 1950s and earlier. But in the 1960s and 1970s, as U.S. automakers neglected their development processes, systems that were once sound and innovative gave way to bureaucracy, internal distrust, and other distractions that brought the companies close to the chimney extreme. In reaction, those companies seem to have swung toward the other end of the spectrum. Results in the short term have been encouraging, but the deficiencies of the committee extreme may well appear soon. Some companies are discovering them already.

The key is to strike the appropriate balance for one's situation. It may be perfectly appropriate in some circumstances to rely almost solely on meetings for communication and problem solving or to abandon standard procedures completely. But such practices are not good for all organizations at all times. They are not panaceas, and they do have significant drawbacks. One must weigh the benefits and drawbacks of a particular practice, including how it contributes to all aspects of integration

How Toyota Avoids Extremes

Chimney Extreme	Toyota Balance	Committee Extreme
Mutual Adjustment		
Little face-to-face contact.	Succinct written reports for most communication.	Reliance on meetings to accomplish tasks.
Predominantly written communication.	Meetings for intensive problem solving.	Predominantly oral communication.
Direct Supervision		
Close supervision of engineers by managers.	Technically astute functional supervisors who mentor, train, and develop their engineers.	Little supervision of engineers.
Large barriers between functions.	Strong functions that are evaluated based on overall system performance.	Weak functional expertise.
Integrative Leadership		
No system design leader.	Project leader as system designer, with limitations on authority.	System design dispersed among team members.

Standard Skills		
No rotation of engineers.	Rotation on intervals that are longer than the typical product cycle, and only to positions that complement the engineers' expertise.	Rotation at rapid and broad intervals.
Standard Work Processes		
New development process with every vehicle.	Standard milestones–project leader decides timing, functions fill in details.	Lengthy, detailed, rigid development schedules.
Complex forms and bureaucratic procedures.	Standard forms and procedures that are simple, devised by the people who use them, and updated as needed.	Making up procedures on each project.
Design Standards		
Obsolete, rigid design standards.	Standards that are maintained by the people doing the work and that keep pace with current company capabilities.	No design standards.

(including integration across projects) and how it affects other parts of the system.

Finally, the success of Toyota's system rides squarely on the shoulders of its people. Successful product development requires highly competent, highly skilled people with a lot of hands-on experience, deep technical knowledge, and an eye for the overall system. When we look at all the things that Toyota does well, we find two foundations of its product-development system: chief engineers using their expertise to gain leadership, and functional engineers using their expertise to reduce the amount of communication, supervision, trial and error, and confusion in the process. All the other coordinating mechanisms and practices serve to help highly skilled designers do their job effectively. By contrast, many other companies seem to aspire to develop systems "designed by geniuses to be run by idiots." Toyota prefers to develop and rely on the skill of its personnel, and it shapes its product-development process around this central idea: people, not systems, design cars.

Originally published in July–August 1998
Reprint 98409

Time-and-Motion Regained

PAUL S. ADLER

Executive Summary

WESTERN MANUFACTURERS have long believed that disciplined, standardized work in a hierarchical environment must inevitably alienate employees, poison labor relations, stifle initiative, lower quality, and hobble a company's capacity to change. This gospel sets up Frederick W. Taylor's time-and-motion studies as the enemy of manufacturing innovation and excellence.

In 1984, General Motors and Toyota set up a joint-venture auto assembly plant (called NUMMI) that turns this creed on its head. NUMMI shows that hierarchy and standardization, with all their known advantages for efficiency, can build on learning rather than coercion and so motivate workers and increase job satisfaction.

NUMMI's production system has two features that distinguish it from most other Japanese-based systems: It is strongly committed to the social context in which work is performed, and it puts an intense focus on standardized work. Social concern is most evident in the no-layoff policy, which commits NUMMI to take various drastic steps, even cutting management salaries, before laying off workers.

As for standardized work, it is workers themselves, not engineers, who analyze jobs, design more efficient procedures, and create a consensus for the new standards. Reduced variability in task performance increases safety, quality, productivity, and flexibility, but by far its most striking advantage is that it gives continuous improvement a specific base to build on. Workers interact with the system by steadily refining it. They make thousands of improvement suggestions, more than 80% of which are implemented. This learning orientation captures workers' desire for excellence and realizes as much as possible of their intelligence and initiative.

STANDARDIZATION IS THE DEATH of creativity.

Time-and-motion regimentation prevents continuous improvement.

Hierarchy suffocates learning.

U.S. manufacturing is in the throes of revolution, and assumptions like these are becoming the new conventional wisdom about work. This new gospel sets up Frederick Winslow Taylor and his time-and-motion studies as the villain. It asserts that quality, productivity, and learning depend on management's ability to free workers from the coercive constraints of bureaucracy. It insists that detailed standards, implemented with great discipline in a hierarchical organization, will inevitably alienate employees, poison labor relations, stifle initiative and innovation, and hobble an organization's capacity to change and to learn.

But what if, as I believe, this new creed is wrong? What if bureaucracy can actually be designed to encourage innovation and commitment? What if standardization, properly understood and practiced, should prove itself a wellspring of continuous learning and motivation?

In Fremont, California, a GM-Toyota joint venture called New United Motor Manufacturing Inc., NUMMI, for short, has succeeded in employing an innovative form of Taylor's time-and-motion regimentation on the factory floor not only to create world-class productivity and quality but also to increase worker motivation and satisfaction. What's more, NUMMI's intensely Taylorist procedures appear to encourage rather than discourage organizational learning and, therefore, continuous improvement.

This outcome seems surprising because for decades our attitudes toward work have been shaped by a chain of reasoning that has led us to expect (and guaranteed that we would get) a vicious circle of escalating managerial coercion and employee recalcitrance. The reasoning runs something like this:

- When tasks are routine and repetitive, efficiency and quality require standardized work procedures.

- High levels of standardization rob jobs of their intrinsic interest, reducing motivation and creativity.

- Demotivating work leads to dysfunctional employee behavior such as absenteeism, high turnover, poor attention to quality, strikes, even sabotage.

- Counterproductive behavior by the work force requires more authoritarian management, more hierarchical layers, and even higher levels of standardization.

In short, Taylorism leads inevitably to workforce discontent and union belligerence, which in turn lead inevitably to higher levels of bureaucratic excess. The organization of work comes to build on the dehumanizing logic of coercion and reluctant compliance. Meanwhile, quality, profits, and job satisfaction all suffer.

NUMMI's experience flies directly in the face of this thinking. That's because the second step in this chain of reasoning is false. Formal work standards developed by industrial engineers and imposed on workers *are* alienating. But procedures that are designed by the workers themselves in a continuous, successful effort to improve productivity, quality, skills, and understanding can humanize even the most disciplined forms of bureaucracy. Moreover, NUMMI shows that hierarchy can provide support and expertise instead of a mere command structure.

What the NUMMI experiment shows is that hierarchy and standardization, with all their known advantages for efficiency, need not build on the logic of coercion. They can build instead on the logic of learning, a logic that motivates workers and taps their potential contribution to continuous improvement.

In practice, NUMMI's "learning bureaucracy" achieves three ends. First, it serves management by improving overall quality and productivity. Second, it serves workers by involving them in the design and control of their own work, increasing their motivation and job satisfaction, and altering the balance of power between labor and management. Third, it serves the interests of the entire organization—management and the work force—by creating a formal system to encourage learning, to capture and communicate innovation, and to institutionalize continuous improvement.

The Worst Plant in the World

NUMMI is housed in what was once the General Motors assembly plant in Fremont, California, 35 miles southeast of San Francisco, which opened in 1963 and manufactured GM trucks and the Chevy Malibu and Century. At the old GM-Fremont plant, work was organized along traditional Taylorist lines, with more than 80 industrial engineers establishing assembly-line norms that management then did its best to impose on the work force, with the predictable results.

Over the years, GM-Fremont came to be what one manager called "the worst plant in the world." Productivity was among the lowest of any GM plant, quality was abysmal, and drug and alcohol abuse were rampant both on and off the job. Absenteeism was so high that the plant employed 20% more workers than it needed just to ensure an adequate labor force on any given day. The United Auto Workers local earned a national reputation for militancy; from 1963 to 1982, wildcat strikes and sickouts closed the plant four times. The backlog of unresolved grievances often exceeded 5,000.

GM-Fremont reached its peak employment of 6,800 hourly workers in 1978. Numbers then declined steadily to a little over 3,000 when GM finally closed the plant in February 1982.

Discussions between GM and Toyota about a possible joint venture began that same year. In February 1983, the two companies reached an agreement in principle to produce a version of the Toyota Corolla, renamed the Nova, at the Fremont plant, using Toyota's production system. GM would be responsible for marketing and sales; Toyota would take on product design, engineering, and daily operations. The new entity, NUMMI, would manufacture and assemble the car. Beginning in 1986, the plant also made Corolla FXs. In 1988, both the Nova and the FX were phased out, and Fremont began building Corollas, Geo Prizms, and, as of late 1991, Toyota trucks.

The two companies' objectives were complementary. GM wanted to learn about Toyota's production system. It also obtained a high-quality subcompact for its Chevrolet division at a time when GM's market share was rapidly eroding. Toyota wanted to help defuse the trade issue by building cars in the United States. To do this, it needed to learn about U.S. suppliers.

Toyota later claimed it had also wanted "to gain experience with American union labor," but at first Toyota wanted nothing to do with the UAW. As it happened, there was no alternative. GM offered them no other facility, and the UAW had de facto control of Fremont. Moreover, GM was afraid of a union backlash at other plants if it tried to set up the joint venture as a nonunion shop.

In September 1983, NUMMI and the union signed a letter of intent recognizing the UAW as sole bargaining agent for the NUMMI labor force, specifying prevailing auto-industry wages and benefits, and stipulating that a majority of the work force would be hired from among the workers laid off from GM-Fremont. In return, the UAW agreed to support the implementation of a new production system and to negotiate a new contract.

NUMMI was formally organized in February 1984. Toyota contributed $100 million in capital, and GM supplied the Fremont plant. Hiring began in May. Every applicant went through three days of production simulations, written examinations, discussions, and interviews. Managers and union officials jointly evaluated applicants for the hourly jobs: team leader and team member. The union also played a role in selecting managers, except for the 16 who came directly from GM and a group of about 30 Toyota managers and production coordinators who came from Japan. The CEO, Tatsuo Toyoda, brought with him the prestige of the company's founding family.

Over the following 20 months, NUMMI hired 2,200 hourly workers—85% from the old GM-Fremont plant, among them the old union hierarchy. (Almost none of GM-Fremont's salaried employees was rehired. In any case, many had long since moved to other GM plants.) Since GM-Fremont had done little hiring for several years before it closed, the average age of the new work force was 41. Most had high school educations. About 26% were Hispanic, 20% black, and 15% female.

The first group of 450 team leaders and the entire NUMMI management team attended a three-week training program at the Toyota plant in Japan—Takaoka—on which NUMMI was modeled. These people then helped to set up the new plant and train workers.

The NUMMI production system required people to work harder than they had at GM-Fremont. Jobs at the old plant occupied an experienced worker about 45 seconds out of 60. NUMMI's norm is closer to 57 seconds out of 60. And because workers have to meet much higher quality and efficiency standards, they have to work not only harder but smarter as well.

By the end of 1986, NUMMI's productivity was higher than that of any other GM facility and more than twice that of its predecessor, GM-Fremont. In fact, NUMMI's productivity was nearly as high as Takaoka's, even though its workers were, on average, ten years older and much less experienced with the Toyota production system. Quality, as rated by internal GM audits, customer surveys, and *Consumer Reports* was much higher than at any other GM plant and, again, almost as high as Takaoka's.

Equally important, absenteeism has dropped from between 20% and 25% at the old GM-Fremont plant to a steady 3% to 4% at NUMMI; substance abuse is a minimal problem; and participation in the suggestion program has risen steadily from 26% in 1986 to 92% in 1991. When GM-Fremont closed its doors, it had more than 2,000 grievances outstanding. As of the end of 1991, some 700 grievances had been filed at NUMMI altogether over the course of eight years. The overall proportion of employees describing themselves as "satisfied" or "very satisfied" has risen progressively to more than 90%.

In 1990, Toyota announced that it would invest $350 million in an additional assembly line to build a Toyota truck for the U.S. market. So NUMMI hired 650 hourly workers on top of the 3,100—plus 400 salaried personnel—already employed. The first trucks rolled off the line in August 1991.

Fear, Selection, Socialization

NUMMI's remarkable turnaround poses an obvious question: How is it possible to convert a plant from worst to best quality and from dismal to superlative productivity over the course of a few months? The most obvious answers are not entirely satisfying.

For example, fear. The GM-Fremont plant closed in 1982, and the people rehired by NUMMI didn't go back to work until 1984. Two years of unemployment can produce a great deal of cooperation. In fact, some NUMMI workers believe management makes deliberate use of the specter of another plant closure as a veiled threat to keep people in line. But the chairman of the union bargaining committee points out that while the old plant's closure obviously made workers more receptive to NUMMI's new approach, a return to old coercive management methods would have produced a rapid return to old antagonistic work-force behavior patterns.

A second possibility is that management weeded out troublemakers in the rehiring process. But in fact NUMMI rehired the entire union hierarchy and many well-known militants. In general, very few applicants were screened out. The union even won a second chance for some who failed drug tests the first time around.

A third answer is that NUMMI made use of a comprehensive socialization process during hiring to instill a new set of values in the new work force. Certainly, NUMMI did its best to shape and alter the attitudes of both workers and managers. For example, the company tried to undercut the customary we-they divisions between workers and management by eliminating special parking and eating facilities for managers and by introducing an identical dress code—uniforms—for everyone. Management also devoted a great deal of attention to each individual hire and welcomed each personally to the company that was going to build "the finest vehicles in America."

However much these three factors—fear of unemployment, selection, and socialization—may have contributed to the final outcome, they do not adequately explain NUMMI's continuing success or its ability to let workers draw improved motivation and greater satisfaction from a system that places them in a more regimented and bureaucratic environment and makes them work harder and faster. The most critical piece of that explanation lies in the production system itself and in the policies and practices that buttress it.

The NUMMI Production System

The idea of a production *system* is itself something of a novelty in many U.S. manufacturing plants. All factories have production techniques, procedures, and policies, but these usually comprise not so much a system as an ad hoc accumulation of responses to changing and often contradictory business and design demands. NUMMI's production system is a finely tuned, superbly integrated whole, refined by Toyota over decades of manufacturing experience.

The basic techniques are familiar at least in name. The assembly line is a just-in-time operation that does away with work-in-progress and makes quality assurance the responsibility of each work station. The application of *kaizen,* or continuous improvement, includes an extraordinarily active suggestion program, constant refinement of procedures, and the designation of special kaizen teams to study individual suggestions or carry out specific improvement projects. Every machine and process is designed to detect malfunctions, missing parts, and improper assemblies automatically. Every job is carefully analyzed to achieve maximum efficiency and quality. Job rotation is standard; workers are cross-trained in all team assignments and then allowed to shift from one task to another. Planned production leveling eliminates variation in daily and weekly schedules.

This system is essentially the same one Toyota uses in Japan, the same one many American manufacturers are now beginning to adopt. But NUMMI's approach is distinctive in two respects: first, its strong commitment to the social context in which work is performed, and, second, its intense focus on standardized work.

In terms of social context, NUMMI seeks to build an atmosphere of trust and common purpose. NUMMI maintains exceptional consistency in its strategies and principles, it carefully builds consensus around important decisions, and it has programs ensuring adequate communication of results and other essential information.

The basic structural unit is the production team, of which NUMMI has approximately 350, each consisting of five to seven people and a leader. The idea is that small teams encourage participative decision making and team bonding. Four teams comprise a group, led by a group leader who represents the first layer of management.

Above and beyond the production teams, the bigger team is everyone—all the workers, team leaders, managers, engineers, and staff in the plant as well as NUMMI's suppliers. Toyota leadership wants workers to understand that the company is not the property of management but of everyone together. In NUMMI's view, the primary purpose and responsibility of the management hierarchy is to support the production teams with problem-solving expertise.

The most substantive expression of this big-team strategy is the no-layoff policy spelled out in NUMMI's collective-bargaining agreement with the union. Recognizing that "job security is essential to an employee's well being," NUMMI agrees "that it will not lay off employees unless compelled to do so by severe economic conditions that threaten the long-term viability of the Company." NUMMI agrees to take such drastic measures as reducing management salaries and assigning previously subcontracted work to bargaining unit employees before resorting to layoffs.

Management sees the no-layoff policy as a critical support for its overall production strategy not only because it reinforces the team culture, but also because it eliminates workers' fear that they are jeopardizing jobs every time they come up with an idea to improve efficiency.

Workers came to trust this no-layoff commitment when in 1988 poor sales of the Nova brought capacity utilization down to around 60%. Workers no longer needed on the assembly line were not laid off but instead assigned to kaizen teams and sent to training classes.

Another important support for NUMMI's team concept is its radically simplified job classification system. Where GM-Fremont had 18 skilled trades classifications, NUMMI has two. Where GM-Fremont had 80 hourly pay rates, at NUMMI all production workers get the same hourly rate—currently $17.85—regardless of their jobs, except that team leaders get an extra 60 cents. There are no seniority-, performance-, or merit-based bonuses. Important as money is, equity is more important still in reducing tensions and resentments.

The second distinctive feature of NUMMI's system is standardization. Typically, American companies approach team empowerment by allowing teams considerable autonomy in how they accomplish tasks. NUMMI, in contrast, is obsessive about standardized work procedures. It sees what one NUMMI manager has called "the intelligent interpretation and application of Taylor's time-and-motion studies" as the principal key to its success. The reference to Taylor may be jarring, but it fits.

Standardized Work . . .

At GM-Fremont, industrial engineers did all time-and-motion analysis and formal job design, and workers tended to view them with resentment or contempt. The problem, as one union official described it, was that management assumed a "divine right" to design jobs however it saw fit. Industrial engineers with no direct experience of the work beyond capsule observation would shut themselves in a room, ponder various potentials of the human body, time the result, and promulgate a task design. Or so it seemed to workers, whom no one ever consulted despite their intimate familiarity with the specific difficulties of the work in question.

Normally, when an industrial engineer presented one of these pedantically designed jobs to a supervisor, the supervisor would politely accept it, then promptly discard it in favor of the more traditional kick-ass-and-take-names technique. The worker, in turn, usually ignored both engineer and foreman and did the job however he or she was able—except, of course, when one of them was looking. If an industrial engineer was actually "observing"—stopwatch and clipboard in hand—standard practice was to slow down and make the work look harder. The entire charade was part of an ongoing game of coercion and avoidance. Multiply this scenario by two shifts and thousands of workers, and the result is anything *but* the rational production of a high-quality car.

At NUMMI, in radical contrast to GM-Fremont, team members themselves hold the stopwatch. They learn the techniques of work analysis, description, and improvement. This change in the design and implementation of standardized work has far-reaching implications for worker motivation and self-esteem, for the balance of power between workers and management, and for the capacity of the company to innovate, learn, and remember.

The job design process itself is relatively simple. Team members begin by timing one another with stopwatches, looking for the safest, most efficient way to do each task at a sustainable pace. They pick the best performance, break it down into its fundamental parts, then explore ways of improving each element. The team then takes the resulting analyses, compares them with those of the other shift at the same work station, and writes the detailed specifications that become the standard work definition for everyone on both teams.

Taking part in the group's analytical and descriptive work involves every team member in a commitment to perform each task identically. In one sense, therefore, standardized work is simply a means of reducing variability in task performance, which may seem a relatively trivial achievement. In fact, however, reduced variability leads to a whole series of interconnected improvements:

- Safety improves and injuries decline because workers get a chance to examine all the possible sources of strain and danger systematically.

- Quality standards rise because workers have identified the most effective procedure for each job.

- Inventory control grows easier, and inventory carrying costs go down because the process flows more smoothly.

- Job rotation becomes much more efficient and equitable, which makes absences less troublesome.

- Flexibility improves because all workers are now industrial engineers and can work in parallel to respond rapidly to changing demands. For example, NUMMI can convert to a new line speed in four to six weeks, a process that might easily have taken six months to a year at GM-Fremont, with its engineers frantically recalculating thousands of tasks and trying to force the new standards on workers. In fact, GM-Fremont never even attempted anything as demanding as a line-speed change. If orders declined, GM-Fremont had to lay off an entire shift. NUMMI's new capacity to alter line speed means, among other things, that the plant can accommodate a drop in orders by slowing production.

- Standardized work also has the overall benefit of giving control of each job to the people who know it best. It empowers the work force. Not surprisingly, NUMMI discovered that workers bought into the process quite readily. As one manager put it, "They understood the technique because it had been done *to* them for years, and they liked the idea because now they had a chance to do it for themselves."

. . . and Continuous Improvement

Yet by far the most striking advantage of standardized work is that it gives continuous improvement a specific base to build on. As one manager put it, "You can't improve a process you don't understand." In this sense, standardization is the essential precondition for learning.

Indeed, standardization is not only a vehicle and a precondition for improvement but also a direct stimulus. Once workers have studied and refined their work procedures, problems with materials and equipment quickly rise to the surface. Moreover, since each worker is now an expert, each work station is now an inspection station—and a center of innovation.

At GM-Fremont, worker suggestions were apt to meet a brick wall of indifference. At NUMMI, engineers and managers are meant to function as a support system rather than an authority system. When a team can't solve a problem on its own, it can seek and get help. When a worker proposes complex innovation, engineers are available to help assess the suggestion and design its implementation.

The difference between traditional Taylorism and the learning-oriented NUMMI version resembles the difference between computer software designed to be "idiot-proof" and the kinds of computer systems that are meant to leverage and enhance their users' capabilities. The first "de-skills" the operator's task to an extent that virtually eliminates the possibility of error, but it also eliminates the operator's ability to respond to unpredictable events, to use the system in novel ways or adapt it to new applications. The idiot-proof system may be easy to use, but it is also static and boring. Leveraging systems make demands on the operator. They take time to learn and require thought and skill to use, but they are immensely flexible, responsive, and satisfying once mastered.

The difference goes deeper yet. At GM-Fremont—where work procedures were designed to be idiot-proof—the relationship between production system and worker was adversarial. Standards and hierarchy were there to coerce effort from reluctant workers. If the sys-

tem functioned as expected and the operator was suffi-
ciently tractable and unimaginative, the two together
could turn out a fair product. There was little the operator could improve on, however, and the role of the system was utterly rigid until it broke down, whereupon
everything stopped until a specialist arrived.

At NUMMI, the relationship of workers to the production system is cooperative and dynamic. Instead of
circumventing user intelligence and initiative, the production system is designed to realize as much as possible
of the latent collaborative potential between the workers
and the system.

Suggestion programs illustrate the two approaches
to organizational technology design. At many companies, suggestion programs are idiot-proof and opaque.
They are designed primarily to screen out dumb ideas,
and the basic review criteria, the identity of the judges,
the status of proposals, and the reasons for rejection
are all a black box as far as the workers are concerned.
Predictably, a lot of these programs sputter along or
die out altogether.

At NUMMI, the program is designed to encourage a
growing flow of suggestions and to help workers see and
understand criteria, evaluators, process, status, and
results. Like a computer system designed to leverage
rather than de-skill, the program helps employees form a
mental model of the program's inner workings. Not surprisingly, workers made more than 10,000 suggestions in
1991, of which more than 80% were implemented.

In systems that de-skill and idiot-proof, technology
controls, indeed dominates, workers. In systems designed
for what experts call usability, the operator both learns
from and "teaches" the technology. Using learned analytical tools, their own experience, and the expertise of

leaders and engineers, workers create a consensual standard that they teach to the system by writing job descriptions. The system then teaches these standards back to workers, who, then, by further analysis, consultation, and consensus, make additional improvements. Continual reiteration of this disciplined process of analysis, standardization, re-analysis, refinement, and restandardization creates an intensely structured system of continuous improvement. And the salient characteristic of this bureaucracy is learning, not coercion.

This learning orientation captures the imagination. People no one had ever asked to solve a problem, workers who never finished high school, men and women who had spent 20 years or more in the auto industry without a single day of off-the-job training found themselves suddenly caught up in the statistical analysis of equipment downtime, putting together Pareto charts. One worker reported that he did literally a hundred graphs before he got one right.

A woman on the safety committee in the body shop described how she applied kaizen techniques to her kitchen at home after a fire on her stove. She analyzed the kitchen layout, installed a fire extinguisher, and relocated her pot tops so she could use them to smother flames. In short, she subjected herself and her home work space to the formal problem-solving procedures she had learned at the NUMMI plant.

The paradoxical feature such stories have in common is their enthusiasm for a form of disciplined behavior that both theory and past practice seem to rule out. This paradox grows from our failure to distinguish between what Taylorist, bureaucratic production systems *can* be and what, regrettably, they have usually been.

The Psychology of Work

The chain of reasoning by which disciplined standardization leads inescapably to coercion, resentment, resistance, and further coercion seems to turn Taylorism and bureaucracy into what sociologist Max Weber called an iron cage. Taylorism and bureaucracy may have a devastating effect on innovation and motivation, the reasoning goes, but their technical efficiency and their power to enforce compliance seem to be the perfect tools for dealing with employees assumed to be recalcitrant. Taylor himself at least occasionally endorsed this coercive view of work. Italics bristling, he once wrote, "It is only through the *enforced* standardization of methods, *enforced* adoption of the best implements and working conditions, and *enforced* cooperation that this faster work can be assured. And the duty of enforcing the adoption of standards and of enforcing this cooperation rests with the *management* alone."

Against this background, it is hardly surprising that most managers and academics, at least in the West, have come to believe that Taylorism and bureaucracy will inevitably alienate workers and squander their human potential. But the psychological assumption underlying this expectation is that workers are incapable of delayed gratification. Managers seem to believe that performance will improve only as work comes more and more to resemble free play—our model of an intrinsically motivating activity. Indeed, it is an elementary axiom of economics that work is something that workers will always avoid.

NUMMI demonstrates the error of imputing infantile psychology to workers. Interviews with NUMMI team members suggest, in fact, that this whole historical accumulation of assumptions obscures three sources of adult motivation that the NUMMI production system successfully taps into:

First, the desire for excellence.

Second, a mature sense of realism.

Third, the positive response to respect and trust.

The first of these—the desire to do a good job, the instinct for workmanship—comes up again and again in conversations with workers. The NUMMI production system and the training that went with it increased both the real competence of workers and their feelings of competence. Workers talk a lot about expertise, pride, and self-esteem. One UAW official named "building a quality product" as one of the strategic goals that the union found most compelling at NUMMI. Perhaps the most striking story about pride in all the interviews came from a team leader:

> *Before, when I saw a Chevy truck, I'd chuckle to myself and think, "You deserve that piece of crap if you were stupid enough to buy one." I was ashamed to say that I worked at the Fremont plant. But when I was down at the Monterey Aquarium a few weekends ago, I left my business card—the grunts even have business cards— on the windshield of a parked Nova with a note that said, "I helped build this one." I never felt pride in my job before.*

The second element of motivation is a mature sense of realism—in this case, the understanding that unless NUMMI constantly improves its performance, competitors will take its market and its workers' jobs. A useful psychological theory cannot assume that workers are so captive to the pleasure principle that their only source of motivation is the immediate pleasure of intrinsically meaningful work. The evidence suggests that at least some of the workers at NUMMI are powerfully motivated by the simple recognition that international competition now forces them to "earn their money the old-fashioned way."

Other things being equal, work that is intrinsically motivating—as opposed to mundane and routine—is better than work that isn't. But workers at NUMMI recognize that other things are *not* equal, and they are realistic in their recognition of having had an unlucky draw in terms of education and opportunity. They see automobile assembly as work that can never have much intrinsic value, but they understand that their own motivation levels can nevertheless vary from strongly negative, at GM-Fremont, to strongly positive, at NUMMI.

"What we have here is not some workers' utopia," said one NUMMI worker. "Working on an assembly line in an automobile factory is still a lousy job. . . . We want to continue to minimize the negative parts of the job by utilizing the new system." Even though this work lacks the kind of intrinsic interest that would bring a worker in on a free Sunday, for example, the difference between the levels of motivation at NUMMI and at GM-Fremont spells the difference between world-class and worst-in-class.

The third explanation of increased motivation is the respect and trust that management shows workers in NUMMI's ongoing operations. For example, when the plant first began operations, the new NUMMI managers responded quickly to requests from workers and union representatives for items like new gloves and floor mats, which surprised workers used to seeing requests like these turn into battles over management prerogative.

After a few months of getting everything they asked for, workers and union representatives started trying to think of ways to reciprocate. Eventually, they decided that chrome water fountains were unnecessary and told management they'd found some plastic ones for half the price. A few weeks later, management upped the ante one more time by giving work teams their own accounts so they could order supplies for team members without prior approval from management. This kind of behavior led workers to conclude that they did indeed share common goals with management.

Power and Empowerment

The NUMMI production system confronts us with a set of formalized procedures that seem designed not primarily as instruments of domination but as elements of productive technique that all participants recognize as tools in their own collective interest. Management *and* labor support the NUMMI system. In fact, the first and overwhelming fact to emerge from interviews is that no one at NUMMI wants to go back to the old GM-Fremont days. Whatever their criticisms and whatever their positions, everyone feels that NUMMI is a far superior work environment.

NUMMI's no-layoff policy, management efforts to build an atmosphere of trust and respect, the NUMMI production system—especially the stimulus of its learning orientation—all help to explain this attitude. Beyond these formal policies, however, there are two more factors that help explain NUMMI's success with workers.

The first of these, as we've seen, is the psychology of work. The final piece of the puzzle has to do with power.

There are two kinds of power to consider: hierarchical power within the organization and the power balance between labor and management. NUMMI takes a distinctive approach to both.

In terms of hierarchical layers, NUMMI is a fairly typical U.S. manufacturing plant, and in this sense, as well as in work-flow procedures, it is a very bureaucratic organization. NUMMI's structure is not flat. It has several well-populated layers of middle management. But consistent with the idea of turning the technologies of coercion into tools for learning, the function of hierarchy at NUMMI is not control but support.

Decisions at NUMMI are made by broad vertical and horizontal consensus. At first glance, decision making appears to be somewhat *more* centralized than at most U.S. factories, but this is because consensus-based decision making draws higher and lower layers into a dialogue, not because higher levels wield greater unilateral control. Both ends of the hierarchical spectrum are drawn into more decision-making discussions than either would experience in a conventional organization.

The contrast with the popular approaches to empowerment is striking. At one U.S. telecommunications company, the model organization today is a plant of 90 workers in self-managed teams, all reporting to a single plant manager. The company's old model included a heavy layer of middle management whose key function was to command and control, so it is easy to understand the inspiring effect of the new approach. But at NUMMI, middle management layers are layers of expertise, not of rights to command, and if middle managers have authority, it is the authority of experience, mastery, and the capacity to coach.

As for the second aspect of power, many observers have assumed that the intense discipline of Toyota-style operations requires complete management control over workers and elimination of independent work-force and union power. But at NUMMI, the power of workers and the union local is still considerable. In some ways, their power has actually increased. In fact, it may be that the NUMMI model has succeeded only *because* of this high level of worker and union power.

What makes the NUMMI production system so enormously effective is its ability to make production problems immediately visible and to mobilize the power of teamwork. Implemented with trust and respect, both these features of the system create real empowerment. Wielded autocratically, they would have the opposite effect. Visible control could easily turn into ubiquitous surveillance. Teamwork could become a means of mobilizing peer pressure. A healthy level of challenge could degenerate into stress and anxiety.

The NUMMI production system thus gives managers enormous potential control over workers. With this potential power ready at hand, and under pressure to improve business performance, there is a real danger that the relationship will sooner or later slide back into the old coercive pattern.

But such a slide would have an immediate and substantial negative impact on business performance, because labor would respond in kind. An alienated work force wipes out the very foundation of continuous improvement and dries up the flow of worker suggestions that fuel it. And the lack of inventory buffers means that disaffected workers could easily bring the whole just-in-time production system to a grinding halt. Alongside workers' positive power to improve quality and efficiency, the system also gives workers an enormous negative power to disrupt production.

In other words, NUMMI's production system increases the power both of management over workers and of workers over management.

A system this highly charged needs a robust governance process in which the voices of management and labor can be clearly heard and effectively harmonized on high-level policy issues as well as on work-team operating issues. The union gives workers this voice.

When, for example, workers felt frustrated by what they saw as favoritism in management's selection of team leaders, the union largely eliminated the problem by negotiating a joint union-management selection process based on objective tests and performance criteria.

As one UAW official put it, "The key to NUMMI's success is that management gave up some of its power, some of its traditional prerogatives. If managers want to motivate workers to contribute and to learn, they have to give up some of their power. If managers want workers to trust them, we need to be 50-50 in making the decision. Don't just make the decision and say, 'Trust me.' "

Union leaders and top management confer regularly on- and off-site to consider a broad range of policy issues that go far beyond the traditional scope of collective bargaining. The union local has embraced the NUMMI concept and its goals. But its ability and willingness to act as a vehicle for worker concerns adds greatly to the long-term effectiveness of the organization.

NUMMI's ability to sustain its productivity, quality, and improvement record now depends on workers' motivation, which rests, in turn, on the perception and reality of influence, control, and equitable treatment. It is in management's own interest that any abuse of management prerogatives should meet with swift and certain penalties. The contribution of labor's positive power depends on the reality of its negative power.

In this way, the union not only serves workers' special interests, it also serves the larger strategic goals of the business by effectively depriving management of absolute domain and helping to maintain management discipline.

Empowerment is a powerful and increasingly popular approach to reinvigorating moribund organizations. The NUMMI case points up two of empowerment's potential pitfalls and suggests ways of overcoming them.

First, worker empowerment degenerates into exploitation if changes at the first level of management are not continuously reinforced by changes throughout the management hierarchy. Strong employee voice is needed to ensure that shop-floor concerns are heard at all levels of management. Without it, workers' new power is little more than the power to make more money for management.

Second, worker empowerment degenerates into abandonment if work teams fail to get the right tools, training in their use, and support in their implementation. Standardized work, extensive training in problem solving, a responsive management hierarchy, and supportive specialist functions are key success factors for empowerment strategies.

Taylorist time-and-motion discipline and formal bureaucratic structures are essential for efficiency and quality in routine operations. But these principles of organizational design need not lead to rigidity and alienation. NUMMI points the way beyond Taylor-as-villain to the design of a truly learning-oriented bureaucracy.

Voices from the Factory Floor: Excerpts from Interviews with Managers, Workers, and Union Officials

Team Leader

I'LL NEVER FORGET when I was first hired by GM many years ago. The personnel manager who hired us got the . . . workers who were starting that day into a room and explained: "You new employees have been hired in the same way we requisition sandpaper. We'll put you back on the street whenever you aren't needed any more." How in the hell can you expect to foster a loyal and productive work force when you start out hearing stuff like that? At NUMMI, the message when we came aboard was "Welcome to the family."

Team Leader

ONCE YOU START WORKING as a real team, you're not just work acquaintances anymore. When you really have confidence in your co-workers, you trust them, you're proud of what you can do together, then you become loyal to them. That's what keeps the absenteeism rate so low here. When I wake up in the morning, I know there's no one out there to replace me if I'm feeling sick or hung over or whatever. . . . At NUMMI, I know my team needs me.

Team Leader

THE AVERAGE WORKER is definitely busier at NUMMI than he was at Fremont. That's the point of the NUMMI production system and the way it ties together standardized work, no inventories, and no quality defects. The work teams at NUMMI aren't like the autonomous teams you read about in other plants. Here we're not autonomous, because we're all tied together really tightly. But it's not like we're just getting squeezed to work harder, because it's the workers who are making the whole thing work—we're the ones that make the standardized work and the *kaizen* suggestions. We run the plant—and if it's not running right, we stop it. At GM-Fremont, we ran only our own little jobs. We'd work really fast to build up a stock cushion so we could take a break for a few minutes to smoke a cigarette or chat with a buddy. That kind of "hurry up and wait" game made work really tiring. There was material and finished parts all over the place, and half of it was defective anyway. Being consistently busy without being hassled and without being overworked takes a lot of the pain out of the job. You work harder at NUMMI, but I swear it, you go home at the end of the day feeling less tired—and feeling a hell of a lot better about yourself!

Team Member

IN OUR STANDARDIZED WORK TRAINING, our teachers told us we should approach our fellow team members and suggest ways to improve their jobs. Hell, do you see me trying that with a team member who's six-foot-four and weighs 250 pounds? You'd be picking me up off the floor if I tried that. . . . Standardized work is a joke as far as I can see. We're supposed to go to management and tell them when we have extra seconds to spare. Why would I do that when all that will happen is that they'll take my spare seconds away and work me even harder than before? I'd rather just do the job the way I'm already comfortable with. I'm no fool.

Department Manager

OUR ASSUMPTION AT NUMMI is that people come to work to do a fair day's work. There are exceptions, and you would be foolish to ignore them. But 90% of people, if you give them a chance to work smarter and improve their jobs, and if they find that by doing that they have created free time for themselves, will spontaneously look for new things to do. I've got hundreds of examples. I don't think that people work harder at NUMMI than in other plants. Not physically anyway. But the mental challenge is much greater.

Team Leader

I DON'T THINK INDUSTRIAL ENGINEERS are dumb. They're just ignorant. Anyone can watch someone else doing a job and come up with improvement suggestions that sound good. . . And it's even easier to come up with the ideal procedure if you don't even bother to watch the worker at work, but just do it from your office, on paper. Almost anything can look good that way. Even when we do our own analysis in our teams, some of the silliest ideas can slip through before we actually try them out.

There's a lot of things that enter into a good job design. . . . The person actually doing the job is the only one who can see all factors. And in the United States, engineers have never had to work on the floor—not like in Japan. So they don't know what they don't know. . . . Today we drive the process, and if we

need help, the engineer is there the next day to work on
it with us.

UAW Official

ONE THING I REALLY LIKE about the Toyota style is that
they'll put in a machine to save you from bending down.
The Toyota philosophy is that the worker should use the
machine and not vice versa. . . . It would be fine if the
robots worked perfectly—and the engineers always seem
to imagine that they will. But they don't, so the worker
ends up being used by the machine. At NUMMI, we just
put in a robot for installing the spare tire—that really helps
the worker, because it was always a hell of a tiring job.
It took awhile, and we had to raise it in the safety meetings and argue about it. And they came through. That
would never happen at GM-Fremont—you never saw
automation simply to help the worker.

UAW Official

IN THE FUTURE WE'RE GOING TO NEED union leaders
with more technical and management knowledge.
We're much more involved now in deciding how the
plant operates. That stretches our capabilities. Management is coming to us asking for our input. . . . The old
approach was much simpler—"You make the damned
decision, and I'll grieve it if I want." Now we need to
understand how the production system works, to take the
time to analyze things, to formulate much more detailed
proposals. This system really allows us to take as much
power as we know what to do with.

UAW Official

NOW WHEN I TRY TO EXPLAIN [NUMMI] to old
UAW buddies from other plants . . . they figure that I'm

forced to say all this stuff because they shut our plant down and I had no choice. They figure going along with the team concept and all the rest was just the price we had to pay to get our jobs back. I explain to them that the plant is cleaner, it's safer, we've got more say on important issues, and we have a real opportunity to build our strength as a union. I explain to them that our members can broaden their understanding of the manufacturing system and build their self-esteem, and that the training we've gotten in manufacturing, problem solving, quality, and so on can help them reach their full potential and get more out of their lives. I explain to them that in a system like this, workers have got a chance to make a real contribution to society—we don't have to let managers do all the thinking. But these guys just don't see it. Maybe it's because they haven't personally experienced the way NUMMI works. Whatever the reason, they just see it all as weakening the union. Someone like Irving Bluestone probably understands what we're doing. He had the idea a long time ago: if the worker has the right to vote for the president of the United States, he ought to have the right to participate in decisions on the shop floor.

Team Member

IN THE OLD DAYS, we had to worry about management playing its games, and the union was there to defend us. But now, with the union taking on its new role, it's not as simple as before, and we have to worry about both the management games and the union games. I don't want the type of union muscle we used to have. You could get away with almost anything in the old plant, because the union would get you off the hook. It was really crazy. But it wasn't productive.

Team Leader

THERE ARE PEOPLE here who will tell you they hate this place. All I say is: actions speak louder than words. If people were disgruntled, there's no way that we'd be building the highest quality vehicle. You wouldn't have a plant that's this clean. You would still have the drug problems we had before. You would still have all the yelling and screaming. You can't force all that. And try this: go into any of the bathrooms, and you'll see there's no graffiti. If people have a problem with their manager, they don't have to tell him on the bathroom wall. They can tell him to his face. And the boss's first words will be: "Why?" Something's happened here at NUMMI. When I was at GM, I remember a few years ago I got an award from my foreman for coming to work for a full 40 hours in one week. A certificate! At NUMMI, I've had perfect attendance for two years.

Originally published in January–February 1998
Reprint 93101

Managing in an Age of Modularity

CARLISS Y. BALDWIN

AND KIM B. CLARK

Executive Summary

MODULARITY IS A FAMILIAR PRINCIPLE in the computer industry. Different companies can independently design and produce components, such as disk drives or operating software, and those modules will fit together into a complex and smoothly functioning product because the module makers obey a given set of design rules.

Modularity in manufacturing is already common in many companies. But now a number of them are beginning to extend the approach into the design of their products and services. Modularity in design should tremendously boost the rate of innovation in many industries as it did in the computer industry.

As businesses as diverse as auto manufacturing and financial services move toward modular designs, the authors say, competitive dynamics will change enormously. No longer will assemblers control the final product: suppliers of key modules will gain leverage and even take on responsibility for design rules. Companies will compete either by specifying the dominant design rules (as Microsoft does) or by producing excellent modules (as disk drive maker Quantum does).

Leaders in a modular industry will control less, so they will have to watch the competitive environment closely for opportunities to link up with other module makers. They will also need to know more: engineering details that seemed trivial at the corporate level may now play a large part in strategic decisions. Leaders will also become knowledge managers internally because they will need to coordinate the efforts of development groups in order to keep them focused on the modular strategies the company is pursuing.

IN THE NINETEENTH CENTURY, railroads fundamentally altered the competitive landscape of business. By providing fast and cheap transportation, they forced previously protected regional companies into battles with distant rivals. The railroad companies also devised management practices to deal with their own complexity and high fixed costs that deeply influenced the second wave of industrialization at the turn of the century.

Today the computer industry is in a similar leading position. Not only have computer companies transformed a wide range of markets by introducing cheap and fast information processing, but they have also led the way toward a new industry structure that makes the best use of these processing abilities. At the heart of their remarkable advance is modularity—building a complex product or process from smaller subsystems that can be designed independently yet function together as a whole. Through the widespread adoption of modular designs, the computer industry has dramatically increased its rate of innovation. Indeed, it is modularity, more than speedy processing and communication or any other technology, that is responsible for the heightened pace of change that managers in the computer industry now face. And strategies based on modularity are the best way to deal with that change.

Many industries have long had a degree of modularity in their production processes. But a growing number of them are now poised to extend modularity to the design stage. Although they may have difficulty taking modularity as far as the computer industry has, managers in many industries stand to learn much about ways to employ this new approach from the experiences of their counterparts in computers.

A Solution to Growing Complexity

The popular and business presses have made much of the awesome power of computer technology. Storage capacities and processing speeds have skyrocketed while costs have remained the same or have fallen. These improvements have depended on enormous growth in the complexity of the product. The modern computer is a bewildering array of elements working in concert, evolving rapidly in precise and elaborate ways.

Modularity has enabled companies to handle this increasingly complex technology. By breaking up a product into subsystems, or *modules,* designers, producers, and users have gained enormous flexibility. Different companies can take responsibility for separate modules and be confident that a reliable product will arise from their collective efforts.

The first modular computer, the System/360, which IBM announced in 1964, effectively illustrates this approach. The designs of previous models from IBM and other mainframe manufacturers were unique; each had its own operating system, processor, peripherals, and application software. Every time a manufacturer introduced a new computer system to take advantage of improved technology, it had to develop software and components specifically for that system while continuing to maintain those for the previous systems. When end users switched to new machines, they had to rewrite all their existing programs, and they ran the risk of losing critical data if software conversions were botched. As a result, many customers were reluctant to lease or purchase new equipment.

The developers of the System/360 attacked that problem head-on. They conceived of a family of computers that would include machines of different sizes suitable for different applications, all of which would use the same instruction set and could share peripherals. To achieve this compatibility, they applied the principle of *modularity in design:* that is, the System/360's designers divided the designs of the processors and peripherals into *visible* and *hidden* information. IBM set up a Central Processor Control Office, which established and enforced the visible overall design rules that determined how the different modules of the machine would work together. The dozens of design teams scattered around the world had to adhere absolutely to these rules. But each team had full control over the hidden elements of design in its module—those elements that had no effect on other modules. (See the sidebar "A Guide to Modularity" at the end of this article.)

When IBM employed this approach and also made the new systems compatible with existing software (by adding "emulator" modules), the result was a huge commercial and financial success for the company and its customers. Many of IBM's mainframe rivals were forced to abandon the market or seek niches focused on customers with highly specialized needs. But modularity also undermined IBM's dominance in the long run, as new companies produced their own so-called plug-compatible modules—printers, terminals, memory, software, and eventually even the central processing units themselves—that were compatible with, and could plug right into, the IBM machines. By following IBM's design rules but specializing in a particular area, an upstart company could often produce a module that was better than the ones IBM was making internally. Ultimately, the dynamic, innovative industry that has grown up around these modules developed entirely new kinds of computer systems that have taken away most of the mainframe's market share.

The fact that different companies (and different units of IBM) were working independently on modules enormously boosted the rate of innovation. By concentrating on a single module, each unit or company could push deeper into its workings. Having many companies focus on the design of a given module fostered numerous, parallel experiments. The module designers were free to try out a wide range of approaches as long as they obeyed the *design rules* ensuring that the modules would fit together. For an industry like computers, in which technological uncertainty is high and the best way to proceed is often unknown, the more experiments and the more flexibility each designer has to develop and test the experimental modules, the faster the industry is able to arrive at improved versions.

This freedom to experiment with product design is what distinguishes modular suppliers from ordinary subcontractors. For example, a team of disk drive designers has to obey the overall requirements of a personal computer, such as data transmission protocols, specifications for the size and shape of hardware, and standards for interfaces, to be sure that the module will function within the system as a whole. But otherwise, team members can design the disk drive in the way they think works best. The decisions they make need not be communicated to designers of other modules or even to the system's architects, the creators of the visible design rules. Rival disk-drive designers, by the same token, can experiment with completely different engineering approaches for their versions of the module as long as they, too, obey the visible design rules.[1]

Modularity Outside the Computer Industry

As a principle of production, modularity has a long history. Manufacturers have been using it for a century or more because it has always been easier to make complicated products by dividing the manufacturing process into modules or *cells*. Carmakers, for example, routinely manufacture the components of an automobile at different sites and then bring them together for final assembly. They can do so because they have precisely and completely specified the design of each part. In this context, the engineering design of a part (its dimensions and tolerances) serves as the visible information in the manufacturing system, allowing a complicated process to be split up among many factories and even outsourced to other suppliers. Those suppliers may experiment with production processes or logistics, but, unlike in the computer industry, they have historically had little or no input into the design of the components.

Modularity is comparatively rare not only in the actual design of products but also in their use. *Modularity in use* allows consumers to mix and match elements to come up with a final product that suits their tastes and needs. For example, to make a bed, consumers often buy bed frames, mattresses, pillows, linens, and covers from different manufacturers and even different retailers. They all fit together because the different manufacturers put out these goods according to standard sizes. Modularity in use can spur innovation in design: the manufacturers can independently experiment with new products and concepts, such as futon mattresses or fabric blends, and find ready consumer acceptance as long as their modules fit the standard dimensions.

If modularity brings so many advantages, why aren't all products (and processes) fully modular? It turns out that modular systems are much more difficult to design than comparable interconnected systems. The designers of modular systems must know a great deal about the inner workings of the overall product or process in order to develop the visible design rules necessary to make the modules function as a whole. They have to specify those rules in advance. And while designs at the modular level are proceeding independently, it may seem that all is going well; problems with incomplete or imperfect modularization tend to appear only when the modules come together and work poorly as an integrated whole.

IBM discovered that problem with the System/360, which took far more resources to develop than expected. In fact, had the developers initially realized the difficulties of ensuring modular integration, they might never have pursued the approach at all because they also underestimated the System/360's market value. Customers wanted it so much that their willingness to pay amply justified IBM's increased costs.

We have now entered a period of great advances in modularity. Breakthroughs in materials science and other fields have made it easier to obtain the deep product knowledge necessary to specify the design rules. For example, engineers now understand how metal reacts under force well enough to ensure modular coherence in body design and metal-forming processes for cars and big appliances. And improvements in computing, of course, have dramatically decreased the cost of capturing, processing, and storing that knowledge, reducing the cost of designing and testing different modules as well. Concurrent improvements in financial markets and innovative contractual arrangements are helping small companies find resources and form alliances to try out experiments and market new products or modules. In some industries, such as telecommunications and electric utilities, deregulation is freeing companies to divide the market along modular lines.

In automobile manufacturing, the big assemblers have been moving away from the tightly centralized design system that they have relied on for much of this century. Under intense pressure to reduce costs, accelerate the pace of innovation, and improve quality, automotive designers and engineers are now looking for ways to parcel out the design of their complex electromechanical system.

The first step has been to redefine the cells in the production processes. When managers at Mercedes-Benz planned their new sport-utility assembly plant in Alabama, for example, they realized that the complexities of the vehicle would require the plant to control a network of hundreds of suppliers according to an intri-

cate schedule and to keep substantial inventory as a
buffer against unexpected developments. Instead of trying to manage the supply system directly as a whole, they
structured it into a smaller set of large production modules. The entire driver's cockpit, for example—including
air bags, heating and air-conditioning systems, the
instrument cluster, the steering column, and the wiring
harness—is a separate module produced at a nearby
plant owned by Delphi Automotive Systems, a unit of
General Motors Corporation. Delphi is wholly responsible for producing the cockpit module according to certain specifications and scheduling requirements, so it
can form its own network of dozens of suppliers for this
module. Mercedes' specifications and the scheduling
information become the visible information that module
suppliers use to coordinate and control the network of
parts suppliers and to build the modules required for
final production.

Volkswagen has taken this approach even further in
its new truck factory in Resende, Brazil. The company
provides the factory where all modules are built and the
trucks are assembled, but the independent suppliers
obtain their own materials and hire their own workforces to build the separate modules. Volkswagen does
not "make" the car, in the sense of producing or assem-
bling it. But it does establish the architecture of the production process and the interfaces between cells, it sets
the standards for quality that each supplier must meet,
and it tests the modules and the trucks as they proceed
from stage to stage.

So far, this shift in supplier responsibilities differs little from the numerous changes in supply-chain management that many industries are going through. By dele-
gating the manufacturing process to many separate
suppliers, each one of which adds value, the assembler

gains flexibility and cuts costs. That amounts to a refinement of the pattern of modularity already established in production. Eventually, though, strategists at Mercedes and other automakers expect the newly strengthened module makers to take on most of the design responsibility as well—and that is the point at which modularity will pay off the most. As modularity becomes an established way of doing business, competition among module suppliers will intensify. Assemblers will look for the best-performing or lowest cost modules, spurring these increasingly sophisticated and independent suppliers into a race for innovation similar to the one already happening with computer modules. Computer-assisted design will facilitate this new wave of experimentation.

Some automotive suppliers are already moving in that direction by consolidating their industry around particular modules. Lear Seating Corporation, Magna International, and Johnson Controls have been buying related suppliers, each attempting to become the worldwide leader in the production of entire car interiors. The big car manufacturers are indirectly encouraging this process by asking their suppliers to participate in the design of modules. Indeed, GM recently gave Magna total responsibility for overseeing development for the interior of the next-generation Cadillac Catera.

In addition to products, a wide range of services are also being modularized—most notably in the financial services industry, where the process is far along. Nothing is easier to modularize than stocks and other securities. Financial services are purely intangible, having no hard surfaces, no difficult shapes, no electrical pins or wires, and no complex computer code. Because the science of finance is sophisticated and highly developed, these services are relatively easy to define, analyze, and split apart. The design rules for financial transactions arise from centuries-old traditions of bookkeeping combined with modern legal and industry standards and the conventions of the securities exchanges.

As a result, providers need not take responsibility for all aspects of delivering their financial services. The tasks of managing a portfolio of securities, for example—selecting assets, conducting trades, keeping records, transferring ownership, reporting status and sending out statements, and performing custody services—can be readily broken apart and seamlessly performed by separate suppliers. Some major institutions have opted to specialize in one such area: Boston's State Street Bank in custody services, for example.

Other institutions, while modularizing their products, still seek to own and control those modules, as IBM tried to control the System/360. For example, Fidelity, the big, mass-market provider of money management services, has traditionally kept most aspects of its operations in-house. However, under pressure to reduce costs, it recently broke with that practice, announcing that Bankers Trust Company would manage $11 billion worth of stock index funds on its behalf. Index funds are a low-margin business whose performance is easily measured. Under the new arrangement, Bankers Trust's index-fund management services have become a hidden module in Fidelity's overall portfolio offerings, much as Volkswagen's suppliers operate as hidden modules in the Resende factory system.

The other result of the intrinsic modularity of financial instruments has been an enormous boost in innovation. By combining advanced scientific methods with high-speed computers, for example, designers can split up securities into smaller units that can then be reconfigured into derivative financial products. Such innovations have made global financial markets more fluid so that capital now flows easily even between countries with very different financial practices.

Competing in a Modular Environment

Modularity does more than accelerate the pace of change or heighten competitive pressures. It also transforms relations among companies. Module designers rapidly move in and out of joint ventures, technology alliances, subcontracts, employment agreements, and financial arrangements as they compete in a relentless race to innovate. In such markets, revenue and profits are far more dispersed than they would be in traditional industries. Even such companies as Intel and Microsoft, which have substantial market power by virtue of their control over key subsets of visible information, account for less of the total market value of all computer companies than industry leaders typically do.

Being part of a shifting modular cluster of hundreds of companies in a constantly innovating industry is different from being one of a few dominant companies in a stable industry. No strategy or sequence of moves will always work; as in chess, a good move depends on the layout of the board, the pieces one controls, and the skill and resources of one's opponent. Nevertheless, the dual structure of a modular marketplace requires managers to choose carefully from two main strategies. A company can compete as an architect, creating the visible information, or design rules, for a product made up of modules. Or it can compete as a designer of modules that conform to the architecture, interfaces, and test protocols of others. Both strategies require companies to understand products at a deep level and be able to predict how modules will evolve, but they differ in a number of important ways.

For an architect, advantage comes from attracting module designers to its design rules by convincing them that this architecture will prevail in the market-place. For the module maker, advantage comes from mastering the hidden information of the design and from superior execution in bringing its module to market. As opportunities emerge, the module maker must move quickly to fill a need and then move elsewhere or reach new levels of performance as the market becomes crowded.

Following the example of Intel and Microsoft, it is tempting to say that companies should aim to control the visible design rules by developing proprietary architectures and leave the mundane details of hidden modules to others. And it is true that the position of architect is powerful and can be very profitable. But a challenger can rely on modularity to mix and match its own capabilities with those of others and do an end-run around an architect.

That is what happened in the workstation market in the 1980s. Both of the leading companies, Apollo Computer and Sun Microsystems, relied heavily on other companies for the design and production of most of the modules that formed their workstations. But Apollo's founders, who emphasized high performance in their product, designed a proprietary architecture based on their own operating and network management systems. Although some modules, such as the microprocessor, were bought off the shelf, much of the hardware was designed in-house. The various parts of the design were highly interdependent, which Apollo's designers believed was necessary to achieve high levels of performance in the final product.

Sun's founders, by contrast, emphasized low costs and rapid time to market. They relied on a simplified, non-proprietary architecture built with off-the-shelf hardware and software, including the widely available UNIX operating system. Because its module makers did not have to design special modules to fit into its system, Sun was free of the investments in software and hardware design Apollo required and could bring products to market quickly while keeping capital costs low. To make up for the performance penalty incurred by using generic modules, Sun developed two proprietary, hidden hardware modules to link the microprocessor efficiently to the workstation's internal memory.

In terms of sheer performance, observers judged Apollo's workstation to be slightly better, but Sun had the cost advantage. Sun's reliance on other module makers proved superior in other respects as well. Many end users relied on the UNIX operating system in other networks or applications and preferred a workstation that ran on UNIX rather than one that used a more proprietary operating system. Taking advantage of its edge in capital productivity, Sun opted for an aggressive strategy of rapid growth and product improvement.

Soon, Apollo found itself short of capital and its products' performance fell further and further behind Sun's. The flexibility and leanness Sun gained through its non-proprietary approach overcame the performance advantages Apollo had been enjoying through its proprietary strategy. Sun could offer customers an excellent product at an attractive price, earn superb margins, and employ much less capital in the process.

However, Sun's design gave it no enduring competitive edge. Because Sun controlled only the two hidden modules in the workstation, it could not lock its cus-

tomers into its own proprietary operating system or
network protocols. Sun did develop original ideas about
how to combine existing modules into an effective
system, but any competitor could do the same since
the architecture—the visible information behind the
workstation design—was easy to copy and could not
be patented.

Indeed, minicomputer makers saw that workstations
would threaten their business and engineering markets,
and they soon offered rival products, while personal
computer makers (whose designs were already extremely
modular) saw an opportunity to move into a higher-
margin niche. To protect itself, Sun shifted gears and
sought greater control over the visible information in its
own system. Sun hoped to use equity financing from
AT&T, which controlled UNIX, to gain a favored role in
designing future versions of the operating system. If Sun
could control the evolution of UNIX, it could bring the
next generation of workstations to market faster than
its rivals could. But the minicomputer makers, which
licensed UNIX for their existing systems, immediately
saw the threat posed by the Sun-AT&T alliance, and they
forced AT&T to back away from Sun. The workstation
market remained wide open, and when Sun stumbled in
bringing out a new generation of workstations, rivals
gained ground with their own offerings. The race was
on—and it continues.

Needed: Knowledgeable Leaders

Because modularity boosts the rate of innovation, it
shrinks the time business leaders have to respond to
competitors' moves. We may laugh about the concept of
an "Internet year," but it's no joke. As more and more

industries pursue modularity, their general managers, like those in the computer industry, will have to cope with higher rates of innovation and swifter change.

As a rule, managers will have to become much more attuned to all sorts of developments in the design of products, both inside and outside their own companies. It won't be enough to know what their direct competitors are doing—innovations in other modules and in the overall product architecture, as well as shifting alliances elsewhere in the industry, may spell trouble or present opportunities. Success in the marketplace will depend on mapping a much larger competitive terrain and linking one's own capabilities and options with those emerging elsewhere, possibly in companies very different from one's own.

Those capabilities and options involve not only product technologies but also financial resources and the skills of employees. Managers engaged with modular design efforts must be adept at forging new financial relationships and employment contracts, and they must enter into innovative technology ventures and alliances. Harvard Business School professor Howard Stevenson has described entrepreneurship as "the pursuit of opportunity beyond the resources currently controlled," and that's a good framework for thinking about modular leadership at even the biggest companies. (See the sidebars "How Palm Computing Became an Architect" and "How Quantum Mines Hidden Knowledge" at the end of this article.)

At the same time that modularity boosts the rate of innovation, it also heightens the degree of uncertainty in the design process. There is no way for managers to know which of many experimental approaches will win out in the marketplace. To prepare for sudden and dramatic changes in markets, therefore, managers need to be able to choose from an often complex array of technologies, skills, and financial options. Creating, watching, and nurturing a portfolio of such options will become more important than the pursuit of static efficiency per se.

To compete in a world of modularity, leaders must also redesign their internal organizations. In order to create superior modules, they need the flexibility to move quickly to market and make use of rapidly changing technologies, but they must also ensure that the modules conform to the architecture. The answer to this dilemma is modularity within the organization. Just as modularity in design boosts innovation in products by freeing designers to experiment, so managers can speed up development cycles for individual modules by splitting the work among independent teams, each pursuing a different submodule or different path to improvement.

Employing a modular approach to design complicates the task of managers who want to stabilize the manufacturing process or control inventories because it expands the range of possible product varieties. But the approach also allows engineers to create families of parts that share common characteristics and thus can all be made in the same way, using, for example, changes in machine settings that are well understood. Moreover, the growing power of information technology is giving managers more precise and timely information about sales and distribution channels, thus enhancing the efficiency of a modular production system.

For those organizational processes to succeed, however, the output of the various decentralized teams (including the designers at partner companies) must be tightly integrated. As with a product, the key to integration in the organization is the visible information. This is where leadership is critical. Despite what many observers of leadership are now saying, the heads of these companies must do more than provide a vision or goals for the decentralized development teams. They must also delineate and communicate a detailed operating framework within which each of the teams must work.

Such a framework begins by articulating the strategy and plans for the product line's evolution into which the work of the development teams needs to fit over time. But the framework also has to extend into the work of the teams themselves. It must, for example, establish principles for matching appropriate types of teams to each type of project. It must specify the size of the teams and make clear what roles senior management, the core design team, and support groups should play in carrying out the project's work. Finally, the framework must define processes by which progress will be measured and products released to the market. The framework may also address values that should guide the teams in their work (such as leading by example). Like the visible information in a modular product, this organizational framework establishes an overall structure within which teams can operate, provides ways for different teams and other groups to interact, and defines standards for testing the merit of the teams' work. Without careful direction, the teams would find it easy to pursue initiatives that may have individual merit but stray from the company's defining concepts.

Just like a modular product that lacks good interfaces between modules, an organization built around decentralized teams that fail to function according to a clear and effective framework will suffer from miscues and delays. Fast changing and dynamic markets—like those for computers—are unforgiving. The well-publicized problems of many computer companies have often been rooted in inadequate coordination of their development teams as they created new products. Less obvious, but equally important, are the problems that arise when teams fail to communicate the hidden information—the knowledge they develop about module technology—with the rest of the organization. That lack of communication, we have found, causes organizations to commit the same costly mistakes over and over again.

To take full advantage of modularity, companies need highly skilled, independent-minded employees eager to innovate. These designers and engineers do not respond to tight controls; many reject traditional forms of management and will seek employment elsewhere rather than submit to them. Such employees do, however, respond to informed leadership—to managers who can make reasoned arguments that will persuade employees to hold fast to the central operating framework. Managers must learn how to allow members of the organization the independence to probe and experiment while directing them to stay on the right overall course. The best analogy may be in biology, where complex organisms have been able to evolve into an astonishing variety of forms only by obeying immutable rules of development.

A CENTURY AGO, the railroads showed managers how to control enormous organizations and masses of capital. In the world fashioned by computers, managers will control less and will need to know more. As modularity drives the evolution of much of the economy, general managers' greatest challenge will be to gain an intimate understanding of the knowledge behind their products. Technology can't be a black box to them because their ability to position the company, respond to market changes, and guide internal innovation depends on this knowledge. Leaders cannot manage knowledge at a distance merely by hiring knowledgeable people and giving them adequate resources. They need to be closely involved in shaping and directing the way knowledge is created and used. Details about the inner workings of products may seem to be merely technical engineering matters, but in the context of intense competition and fast changing technology, the success of whole strategies may hinge on such seemingly minor details.

A Guide to Modularity

MODULARITY IS A STRATEGY for organizing complex products and processes efficiently. A *modular* system is composed of units (or modules) that are designed independently but still function as an integrated whole. Designers achieve modularity by partitioning information into *visible design rules* and *hidden design parameters*. Modularity is beneficial only if the partition is precise, unambiguous, and complete.

The visible design rules (also called *visible information*) are decisions that affect subsequent design decisions. Ideally, the visible design rules are established early in a design process and communicated broadly to those involved. Visible design rules fall into three categories:

- An *architecture*, which specifies what modules will be part of the system and what their functions will be.

- *Interfaces* that describe in detail how the modules will interact, including how they will fit together, connect, and communicate.

- *Standards* for testing a module's conformity to the design rules (can module X function in the system?) and for measuring one module's performance relative to another (how good is module X versus module Y?).

Practitioners sometimes lump all three elements of the visible information together and call them all simply "the architecture," "the interfaces," or "the standards."

The hidden design parameters (also called *hidden information*) are decisions that do not affect the design beyond the local module. Hidden elements can be chosen late and changed often and do not have to be communicated to anyone beyond the module design team.

How Palm Computing Became an Architect

IN 1992, Jeff Hawkins founded Palm Computing to develop and market a handheld computing device for the consumer market. Having already created the basic software for handwriting recognition, he intended to concentrate on refining that software and developing related applications for this new market. His plan was to rely on partners for the basic architecture, hardware, operating system software, and marketing. Venture capitalists funded Palm's own development. The handwriting recognition software became the key hidden module around which a consortium of companies formed to produce the complete product.

Sales of the first generation of products from both the consortium and its rivals, however, were poor, and Palm's partners had little interest in pursuing the next generation. Convinced that capitalizing on Palm's ability to connect the device directly to a PC would unlock the potential for sales, Hawkins and his chief executive, Donna Dubinsky, decided to shift course. If they couldn't get partners to develop the new concept, they would handle it themselves—at least the visible parts, which included the device's interface protocols and its operating system. Palm would have to become an architect, taking control of both the visible information and the hidden information in the handwriting recognition module. But to do so, Hawkins and Dubinsky needed a partner with deeper pockets than any venture capital firm would provide.

None of the companies in Palm's previous consortium was willing to help. Palm spread its net as far as US Robotics, the largest maker of modems. US Robotics was so taken with the concept for and development of Palm's product that it bought the company. With that backing, Palm was able to take the product into full production and get the marketing muscle it needed. The result was the Pilot, or what Palm calls a Personal Connected Organizer, which has been a tremendous success in the marketplace. Palm remains in control of the operating system and the handwriting recognition software in the Pilot but relies on other designers for hardware and for links to software that runs on PCs.

Palm's strategy with the Pilot worked as Hawkins and Dubinsky had intended. In order for its architecture to be accepted by customers and outside developers, Palm had to create a compelling concept that other module makers would accept, with attractive features and pricing, and bring the device to market quickly. Hawkins's initial strategy—to be a hidden-module producer while partners delivered the architecture—might have worked with a more familiar product, but the handheld-computer market was too unformed for it to work in that context. So, when the other members of the consortium balked in the second round of the design process, Palm had to take the lead role in developing both the proof of concept and a complete set of accessible design rules for the system as a whole.

We are grateful to Myra Hart for sharing with us her ongoing research on Palm. She describes the company in detail in her cases "Palm Computing, Inc. (A)," HBS case no. 396245, and "Palm Pilot 1995," HBS case no. 898090.

How Quantum Mines Hidden Knowledge

QUANTUM CORPORATION began in 1980 as a maker of 8-inch disk storage drives for the minicomputer market. After the company fell behind as the industry shifted to 5.25-inch drives, a team led by Stephen M. Berkley and Dave Brown rescued it with an aggressive strategy, applying their storage expertise to developing a 3.5-inch add-on drive for the personal computer market. The product worked, but competing in this sector required higher volumes and tighter tolerances than Quantum was used to. Instead of trying to meet those demands internally, Berkley and Brown decided to keep the company focused on technology and to form an alliance with Matsushita-Kotobuki Electronics Industries (MKE), a division of the Matsushita Group, to handle the high-volume, high-precision manufacturing. With the new alliance in place, Quantum and MKE worked to develop tightly integrated design capabilities that spanned the two companies. The products resulting from those processes allowed Quantum to compete successfully in the market for drives installed as original equipment in personal computers.

Quantum has maintained a high rate of product innovation by exploiting modularity in the design of its own products and in its own organization. Separate, small teams work on the design and the production of each submodule, and the company's leaders have developed an unusually clear operating framework within which to coordinate the efforts of the teams while still freeing them to innovate effectively.

In addition to focusing on technology, the company has survived in the intensely competitive disk-drive industry by paying close attention to the companies that assemble personal computers. Quantum has become the preferred supplier for many of the assemblers because its careful attention to developments in the visible information for disk drives has enabled its drives to fit seamlessly into the assemblers' systems. Quantum's general managers have a deep reservoir of knowledge about both storage technology and the players in the sector, which helps them map the landscape, anticipating which segments of the computer market are set to go into decline and where emerging opportunities will arise. Early on, they saw the implications of the Internet and corporate intranets, and with help from a timely purchase of Digital Equipment Corporation's stagnating storage business, they had a head start in meeting the voracious demand for storage capacity that has been created by burgeoning networks. Despite what some observers might see as a weak position (because the company must depend on the visible information that other companies give out)

Quantum has prospered, recently reporting strong profits
and gains in stock price.

*We are grateful to Steven Wheelwright and Clayton Christensen for sharing with
us their ongoing research on Quantum. They describe the company in more
detail in their case "Quantum Corp.: Business and Product Teams," HBS case
no. 692023.*

Note

1. Practical knowledge of modularity has come largely from
the computer industry. The term *architecture* was first
used in connection with computers by the designers of the
System/360: Gene M. Amdahl, Gerrit A. Blaauw, and Frederick P. Brooks, Jr., in "Architecture of the IBM Sys-
tem/360," *IBM Journal of Research and Development,* April
1964, p. 86. The scientific field of computer architecture
was established by C. Gordon Bell and Allen Newell in
Computer Structures: Readings and Examples (New York:
McGraw-Hill, 1971). The principle of *information hiding*
was first put forward in 1972 by David L. Parnas in "A
Technique for Software Module Specification with Examples," *Communications of the ACM,* May 1972, p. 330. The
term *design rules* was first used by Carver Mead and Lynn
Conway in *Introduction to VLSI Systems* (Reading, Massachusetts: Addison-Wesley, 1980). Sun's architectural innovations, described in the text, were based on the work of
John L. Hennessy and David A. Patterson, later summarized in their text *Computer Architecture: A Quantitative
Approach* (San Mateo, California: Morgan Kaufman Pub-
lishers, 1990).

Originally published in September–October 1997
Reprint 97502

Lean Consumption

JAMES P. WOMACK AND DANIEL T. JONES

Executive Summary

DURING THE PAST 20 YEARS, the real price of most consumer goods has fallen worldwide, the variety of goods and the range of sales channels offering them have continued to grow, and product quality has steadily improved. So why is consumption often so frustrating? It doesn't have to be—and shouldn't be—the authors say. They argue that it's time to apply lean thinking to the processes of consumption—to give consumers the full value they want from goods and services with the greatest efficiency and the least pain.

Companies may think they save time and money by off-loading work to the consumer but, in fact, the opposite is true. By streamlining their systems for providing goods and services, and by making it easier for customers to buy and use those products and services, a growing

171

number of companies are actually lowering costs while saving everyone time. In the process, these businesses are learning more about their customers, strengthening consumer loyalty, and attracting new customers who are defecting from less user-friendly competitors.

The challenge lies with the retailers, service providers, manufacturers, and suppliers that are not used to looking at total cost from the standpoint of the consumer and even less accustomed to working with customers to optimize the consumption process.

Lean consumption requires a fundamental shift in the way companies think about the relationship between provision and consumption, and the role their customers play in these processes. It also requires consumers to change the nature of their relationships with the companies they patronize.

Lean production has clearly triumphed over similar obstacles in recent years to become the dominant global manufacturing model. Lean consumption, its logical companion, can't be far behind.

OVER THE PAST 20 YEARS, the real price of most consumer goods has fallen worldwide, even as the variety of goods and the range of sales channels offering them have continued to grow. Meanwhile, product quality—in the sense of durability and number of delivered defects—has steadily improved.

So, if consumers have access to an ever-growing range of products at lower prices, with fewer lemons, and from more formats, why is consumption often so frustrating? Why do we routinely encounter the custom-built computer that refuses to work with the printer, the other computers in the house, and the network software? Why does the simple process of getting the car fixed require countless loops of miscommunication, travel, waiting, and defective repairs? Why does the diligent shopper frequently return from a store stocking thousands of items without having found the one item that was wanted? And why is this tiresome process of consumption backed up by help desks and customer support centers that neither help nor support? In short, why does consumption—which should be easy and satisfying—require so much time and hassle?

It doesn't have to—and shouldn't. Companies may think that they save time and money by off-loading work to customers, making it the customer's problem to get the computer up and running, and wasting the customer's time. In fact, however, the opposite is true. By streamlining the systems for providing goods and services, and making it easier for customers to buy and use them, a growing number of companies are actually lowering costs while saving everyone's time. In the process, these businesses are learning more about their customers, strengthening consumer loyalty, and attracting new customers who defect from less user-friendly competitors.

What these companies are doing has a familiar feel: Just as businesses around the world have embraced the principles of lean production to squeeze inefficiency out of manufacturing processes, these innovative companies are streamlining the processes of consuming. In the early 1990s we popularized the term *lean production* to describe the ultra-efficient process management of our exemplar firm, Toyota. We believe it is now time to recognize *lean consumption* as its necessary and inevitable complement.

"But surely," you say, "when it comes to consumption, less can't be more." Actually it can be, for both consumer and provider. Lean consumption isn't about reducing the amount customers buy or the business they bring. Rather, it's about providing the full value that consumers desire from their goods and services, with the greatest efficiency and least pain.

The key word here is "process." Think about consumption not as an isolated moment of decision about purchasing a specific product, but as a continuing process linking many goods and services to solve consumer problems. When a person buys a home computer, for example, this is not a onetime transaction. The individual has embarked on the arduous process of researching, obtaining, integrating, maintaining, upgrading, and, finally, disposing of this purchase. For producers and providers (whether employees, managers, or entrepreneurs), developing lean consumption processes requires determining how to configure linked business activities, especially across firms, to meet customer needs without squandering their own—or the consumer's—time, effort, and resources.

The way to do this is to tightly integrate and streamline the processes of provision and consumption. The challenge is not simply logistical: Lean consumption requires a fundamental shift in the way retailers, service providers, manufacturers, and suppliers think about the relationship between provision and consumption, and the role their customers play in these processes. It also requires consumers to change the nature of their relationships with the companies they patronize. Customers and providers must start collaborating to minimize total cost and wasted time and to create new value.

That may seem like a doubtful proposition. But some companies—along with their customers—have started the culture shift that will make lean consumption possible. And they're finding that everybody wins.

Why Lean Consumption Now?

While lean consumption would be a sensible idea in any era, we see several convergent trends that we think make it inevitable and, indeed, a competitive necessity now.

With the regulated economy steadily contracting, consumers have a broader range of decisions to make, from how to invest retirement funds, to what telecommunications provider to use, to what airline to fly at what price. At the same time, they must cope with a growing profusion of choices as producers relentlessly customize their offerings, pursue product niches, and increase their sales channels.

In this demanding environment, information technology is steadily blurring the distinction between consumption and production. Consumers are doing increasing amounts of unpaid work on behalf of providers, such as entering data into Web-based order forms and tracking the progress of their own orders. And these consumers are spending more and more time and energy to obtain and maintain the computers, printers, PDAs, and other technological tools needed to solve routine problems—for themselves *and* for providers.

This growing burden on consumers might be sustainable if not for the changes consumers themselves are undergoing. Household configurations in every advanced economy are transforming in ways that create additional time pressures and energy drains. Two-wage-earner and single-parent households, where no one has time to manage consumption, are increasingly common; and aging populations are confronted with an expanding array of choices but have declining energy to address them.

Collectively, these trends give rise to the consumer's emerging dilemma of more choices to make and products to manage with decreasing time and energy. Yet the situation also creates a major opportunity for providers.

The Principles of Lean Consumption

The concepts underlying lean consumption boil down to six simple principles that correspond closely with those of lean production. (For more on these principles, see our book *Lean Thinking.*)

1. Solve the customer's problem completely by insuring that all the goods and services work, and work together.

2. Don't waste the customer's time.

3. Provide exactly *what* the customer wants.

4. Provide what's wanted exactly *where* it's wanted.

5. Provide what's wanted where it's wanted exactly *when* it's wanted.

6. Continually aggregate solutions to reduce the customer's time and hassle.

Let's examine these principles one at a time.

SOLVE THE CUSTOMER'S PROBLEM COMPLETELY BY INSURING THAT ALL THE GOODS AND SERVICES WORK, AND WORK TOGETHER

Customers obtain goods and services to solve problems in their lives. But they don't acquire them in a single transaction. Instead they search for, obtain, install, integrate, maintain, and dispose of them over an extended period—which is a lot more complicated. We don't just buy a car or a home in an hour to solve our mobility and shelter problems. Rather, we search at length, find the right item, purchase it, and begin immediately to maintain, repair, and upgrade it over an extended period as our needs change.

This complex process rarely goes smoothly. Consider personal computing, which now involves your camera, your PDA, and your phones. Most of us are less interested in the specific features of all these items than providers seem to think. What we really want is for everything (hardware, software, and support services) to work together reliably and seamlessly with minimal drain on our time and emotions. Yet we struggle endlessly with multiple providers of goods and services for our information and communication problems, all of which require our continuous unpaid management.

Why is this? Because providers, instead of working together to perfect the entire consumption process, have created an enormous "failure industry" of help lines and service desks to deal with their individual piece of the solution. Their objective has been ever-greater efficiency (in terms of their own resources) at patching recurring customer problems. Their management goal has been to minimize the time needed to get the customer off the line while avoiding the hard work of getting to the root cause of the problem.

Lean consumption principles suggest a radically different approach. Rather than assigning the least knowledgeable personnel to deal repetitively (but "efficiently") with the same customer problems, a lean provider deploys highly trained personnel who not only solve the customer's specific problem but also identify its systemic source. Management can then put permanent fixes in place, integrating the various elements of the solution, so that consumers no longer need to complain.

This approach has been pursued brilliantly by Fujitsu Services, a leading global provider of outsourced customer service. Companies that contract with Fujitsu to manage their in-house IT help desks find that the number of calls their desks receive about a recurring problem inside the company—say malfunctioning printers—often falls to near zero. What Fujitsu does is identify and fix the *source* of the problem—for example, replace the flawed printers with new ones fit for the particular purpose. By seeking the root cause of the problem somewhere up the value stream (often involving multiple companies), Fujitsu has pioneered a way to eliminate it. (See the sidebar "Solving Problems at the Source" at the end of this article.)

DON'T WASTE THE CUSTOMER'S TIME

Providers typically send a very clear message to customers: "Your time has no value." Just think of when you last had your car repaired. You called to make an appointment, took your vehicle to a dealer, went through numerous queues to explain the problem, arranged for a loaner vehicle or a ride to your destination, and then waited for the dreaded call with the diagnosis and cost of the repair. When you went to pick up the vehicle, you may have found that it wasn't ready. Or you may have waited in several queues (again) to pay for and collect the car, only to discover later that the repair had not been done right. (Surveys show that car repairs are done correctly and on time only six times out of ten.) The dealer squandered your valuable time—and goodwill.

The lean provider takes a different approach by looking at the problem from the standpoint of the customer and drawing a "consumption map" of all the steps in the repair process. Then, in each instance where the customer is forced to expend time for no return in value, the provider asks how the system can be reconfigured to eliminate wasted time.

Most managers instinctively assume that this will raise their costs, but the reality is just the opposite. Purging inefficiency from the "provision stream"—the steps needed to create and deliver goods or services—solves providers' problems even as it helps customers. All those endless queues entail needless work for staff, and reworking jobs done wrong is even more expensive. By marrying a lean provision stream to a lean consumption stream (all the actions that must be taken by the consumer to acquire goods or services), providers can usually reduce their costs—and lower prices to consumers.

Skeptical? Take at look at Grupo Fernando Simão (GFS), a family-owned automobile dealer group based in Oporto, Portugal. GFS is the third-largest dealer group in Portugal, with 900 employees and group sales now more than $400 million. Since 1999, the company has introduced lean provision and consumption practices throughout its entire business. By prediagnosing every car repair whenever possible, scheduling to eliminate queues, standardizing repair processes, and introducing other lean practices, GFS has removed many wasteful steps, increased the speed at which customers and vehicles move through the system, and reduced the total cost to the company of the typical repair by 30%.

This approach yields more than just a cost savings for GFS: It's a boon for customers. The prices customers pay for repairs have fallen—especially in terms of wasted time—and most jobs are now fixed right the first time.

Before these changes, a customer could expect to spend about two hours searching for a repair shop, making an appointment, getting the car to the dealer, negotiating the repair, and collecting the vehicle at the end of the process. GFS's lean repair process has cut customers' time commitments almost by half—to an average of 69 minutes. As a result, GFS has climbed from near the bottom of the car manufacturers' customer-service rankings to the top and has dramatically increased its share of the service business for vehicles it sells. (See the exhibit "Drawing a Lean Consumption Map.")

PROVIDE EXACTLY *WHAT* THE CUSTOMER WANTS

You may think that if current consumption systems do anything well it is to get customers the exact items they want. Not true. For example, the average item in a typical grocery store is in stock at the right location on the shelf only 92% of the time (this is called the "level of service"). Given that the average shopper has 40 items on a list, multiply the probabilities of finding each of the 40 items together and it's apparent that obtaining all of the items in the same shopping trip will happen only one time in 28. You can buy substitutes, or make additional trips, or change what you plan to eat, but the store is not giving you exactly what you want.

Shoe stores don't do any better. By relocating most production for North America and Europe to Southeast Asia and putting retailers on 150-day order windows, the shoe industry has created a marvel of low cost at the factory gate in combination with an extraordinary array of styles (about half of which only endure for one three-month selling season). But suppose you want the size nine "Wonder Wings" in gray? The chances are only 80%

(an industry average) that they will be in stock; and there is a good possibility (because of the long order window) that they will never be in stock again. Not to worry, though. There are millions of size nine Wonder Wings in pink available and many more on the way because the order flow, once turned on, cannot be turned off and the replenishment cycle is so long. As a result, the shoe industry fails to get one customer in five the product he or she actually wants, while it remainders 40% of total production (pink Wonder Wings, for example) through secondary channels at much lower revenues.

There will certainly be differences among industries in the difficulty of implementing lean consumption. But even in those where lean provision seems impractical, there are likely to be practical, if counterintuitive, solutions. Consider that Nike can now profitably deliver even customized bags overnight anywhere in North America. How? By—of all things—locating manufacturing in California. (See the sidebar "Locating for Lean Provision" at the end of this article.)

Whatever the industry, the lean provider's approach has a common theme: pull. Rather than infrequently ordering large numbers of items based on very sophisticated centralized forecasts (which are almost always wrong), the lean provider puts in place rapid replenishment systems that quickly restock exactly what a customer has just pulled from the shelf. This is not just a warehousing problem. It's a total-system issue of multiple replenishment loops running all the way back to raw materials. These loops permit a business to quickly restock at every level what the next downstream customer actually wants, as shown by what a previous customer just used.

Tesco, a UK-based retailer, is the world leader in applying these principles and is now approaching a

Drawing a Lean Consumption Map

Mapping the steps in a production and consumption process is the best way to see opportunities for improvement. A map can reveal how broken processes waste providers' and consumers' time and money.

Here's how Grupo Fernando Simão (GFS), a Portuguese automobile dealer group, discovered the inefficiencies in its processes. First, the company looked at consumption. It listed the steps a typical consumer takes to get a car fixed—from searching for a repair shop to arriving home with the vehicle repaired—and the time required for each. Then GFS drew boxes representing the eight steps it identified, sized each box in proportion to the time needed to complete the corresponding task, and shaded in the value-creating time. The company also collected data on the percentage of jobs done right the first time and on time.

GFS found that these consumption steps took the average consumer a total of 120 minutes. And, because dealers often couldn't do repairs on the day they received the car—either because they didn't have time after diagnosing the problem or because they lacked necessary parts, tools, or knowledge—almost half of the customers' time was wasted. What's more, only 60% of the jobs were completed on time.

Next, GFS mapped the 25 steps in its provision process, adding arrows to show where these provision steps interacted with the steps in the consumption process. The group discovered that the provision steps took 207 minutes of paid time, only 27% of which created any value for the customer. A closer look revealed that technicians, the sole creators of customer value, were creating value during only 45% of their paid work time. Not impressive. (See "Car Repair Before Lean Processes.")

Using this map, GFS eliminated unnecessary steps in both the provision and consumption processes. The gains for GFS and its customers become clearly visible when we look at how the process works today (see "Car Repair After Lean Processes").

Here, GFS leverages its ongoing relationship with customers, eliminating the need for them to search for a new repair shop because of dissatisfaction with a previous repair. GFS prediagnoses the problem by phone whenever possible and confirms the diagnosis as soon as the car arrives. If customers can wait a few moments, they can authorize the repair work right then and avoid the extra phone call. The dealers have also smoothed the work flow by carefully scheduling arrivals to eliminate queues and passing work directly to the technician, with no handoffs. In addition, they have minimized the technician's time by leveling work flow and separating jobs according to their complexity and the time required to complete them. Parts and tools are prekitted and delivered to the technician in the service bay just as needed. And common repair tasks are standardized to reduce time spent as well as to increase the chance of getting the work done correctly and on time.

These gains create a win-win situation. Customers' time is no longer wasted and GFS can handle a greater volume of business. GFS's technicians are now creating value during 78% of their work time and they complete nearly twice as many jobs per day. More jobs are done right the first time, so fewer cars are brought back for a second visit. As a result, GFS requires a smaller support staff and needs only one-quarter the number of loaner cars.

(continued)

Car Repair Before Lean Processes

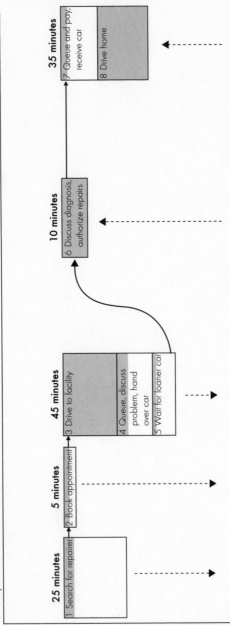

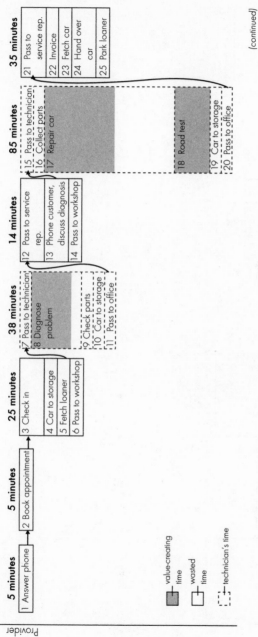

(continued)

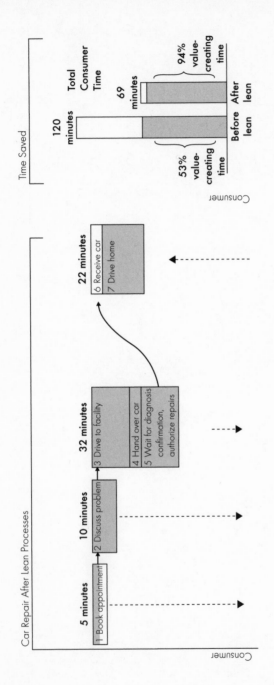

Car Repair After Lean Processes

5 minutes
1 Book appointment

10 minutes
2 Discuss problem

32 minutes
3 Drive to facility
4 Hand over car
5 Wait for diagnosis confirmation, authorize repairs

22 minutes
6 Receive car
7 Drive home

Consumer

Time Saved

Total Consumer Time

120 minutes

69 minutes

Before lean

After lean

53% value-creating time

94% value-creating time

Consumer

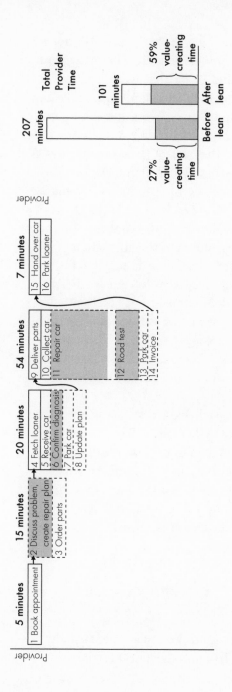

level of service of more than 96%. That's still not good
enough to get all customers exactly what they want,
but it's a big leap—and proof that lean production
principles can support lean consumption.

How does Tesco do it? By replenishing every store
continuously, over a 24-hour day, to eliminate the need
to hold stock either at the back of the store (as does Wal-
Mart) or in high-bay storage (like Home Depot). Tesco
reorders from key suppliers that produce—in a matter
of hours—items that have just been purchased. What's
more, Tesco picks up directly from suppliers' shipping
docks at precise times and takes the goods to regional
distribution centers where fresh products and fast-
moving items are cross docked onto vehicles delivering
to stores. In a further lean innovation, Tesco satisfies
Web-shopping orders by having store personnel fulfill
orders from the shelves during lulls. This process has
reduced personnel costs, avoided the cost of separate
warehouses for Web orders, and made Tesco the world's
largest Internet grocer.

Lean techniques have helped Tesco to grow its share
rapidly and become the UK's market leader in groceries,
fueling its global expansion in Eastern Europe and
East Asia as well. They have also allowed the grocer to
increase customer satisfaction and loyalty by giving
shoppers what they want (and, as we shall see, by providing it where and when they want it)—without wasting
their time.

PROVIDE WHAT'S WANTED EXACTLY *WHERE* IT'S WANTED

Conventional wisdom holds that customers usually
obtain needed items from a single format (the price-

conscious suburban shopper goes to Costco or Sam's Club; the time-pressed urban professional goes to Trader Joe's). But the conventional wisdom is wrong. Balancing many considerations, chief among them price and convenience, most of us use a variety of formats to get what we want as our circumstances change. We make the occasional trip to Costco for bulk items, the weekly trip to the standard supermarket for its wide selection of groceries, and several stops at the convenience store for the little things we missed, and we order out for home delivery when time's especially tight or we're just exhausted. By using different formats depending on circumstances, we minimize our total cost of consumption: the sum of prices we pay for products plus the time and effort expended to obtain them. In this equation, typically, price goes up as time and hassle decrease; we pay— sometimes a lot—for convenience.

Imagine, though, a provision process that maximizes convenience while keeping prices nearly uniform across formats and preserving retailers' margins. In fact, this is possible if one fulfillment channel can supply every format. That's because the cost to the provider of the products entering its channel from suppliers depends predominantly on the buying power of the channel operator rather than on scale economies in larger bulk orders or scale advantages in larger stores.

For instance, the reason Wal-Mart sells hammers more cheaply than the corner hardware store isn't that the scale of Wal-Mart's order reduces hammer production costs or that the store's size significantly reduces its costs. It's because the scale of Wal-Mart's order causes the hammer maker to accept a low selling price in return for volume, and Wal-Mart passes on this savings to its customers.

The opportunity is ripe for large retailers using lean logistics techniques to offer a complete range of formats with uniform pricing to serve every customer need. Tesco is already doing this. It has created a full complement of formats ranging from local convenience stores (Tesco Express), to midsize stores in town centers (Tesco Metro), to standard-size supermarkets in the suburbs (Tesco Superstore), to hypermarkets on the periphery (Tesco Extra), to Web-based shopping (Tesco.com). By integrating the fulfillment channel behind all these formats, Tesco is answering an expanded array of consumption needs.

One result of this efficient channel sharing is that Tesco seems to be the only grocer making money on Web-based grocery shopping while continually increasing sales volume. Another, more provocative consequence is that all of the goods entering this unified fulfillment channel benefit from the same purchasing power: The tube of toothpaste going to the tiny Tesco Express outlet costs Tesco the same amount to buy from the supplier as the tube going to the vast Tesco Extra store, and the fulfillment cost is very nearly the same as well. This strongly suggests that the age of mass consumption retailing, in which the industry keeps heading toward ever larger formats, is coming to an end. Why drive miles to a "big box" if the items you want are available nearby from a smaller format at the same prices?

Perhaps the biggest benefit Tesco gains from this approach is that its customers are no longer strangers. By offering loyalty cards that are accepted at all formats, Tesco has begun to harvest invaluable data about the entire purchasing pattern of the 12 million UK customers in its loyalty program, who account for 80% of

Tesco's sales revenue. This information is now being used to put the right items in the right stores and to target the right customers with the right promotional offers.

With Tesco's multiple-format model, customers can get what they want where they want it, and at a nearly uniform price; and the retailer captures additional consumer spending—and loyalty.

PROVIDE WHAT'S WANTED WHERE IT'S WANTED EXACTLY *WHEN* IT'S WANTED

Most consumers have been trained to believe that goods and services are purchased on impulse. And for small items—the latest DVD release, for example—this may be true. *When* we want them is right now. However, for most items—and in particular for major durable goods, which account for the bulk of our spending—most of us continually plan ahead. We still want the goods when we want them, but that date is often some ways off.

Think about your household vehicles. Do you suddenly decide to buy a new car while driving past a dealer? Probably not. But you probably are contemplating a future purchase even as you read this: You know that you can trade your boring van for a two-door roadster as soon as you haul the youngest child to college next fall, and the SUV will reach a point of questionable reliability by the end of next summer.

Imagine that you could get a customized product for a reduced price simply by sharing your plans with a producer and ordering in advance. This purchasing model already works well for services such as vacation cruises, where advance ticket purchases are not only cheaper but can guarantee a preferred (in a sense, "customized") room. And it could work for consumer goods and a broad range of services—if producers would only listen to you.

But most current interactions actually penalize the customer for planning ahead. For example, if you ask to special order a specific vehicle for delivery sometime in the future, the dealer will be frustrated that you don't want one of the vehicles already in inventory and will try to steer you to available stock through price discounts. And if you insist on ordering ahead, you will pay a penalty when the dealer refuses to budge on price. This situation is bad for both consumers and producers. It thwarts customers' desire to get exactly what they want when they want it, and it increases the producers' production and distribution costs. Producers incur these extra expenses because they can't accurately predict the total volume of products that will be wanted at a specific time or the mix of features each customer will seek. As a result, they must keep extra production capacity available, keep large inventories of finished units and parts on hand, or both.

Most of us do plan ahead for large, durable purchases and would be willing to share our plans with the producer in return for getting exactly what we want at a future date with a discount. And those who absolutely must have a specific product (standard shift, purple paint) right now are usually willing to pay a premium for it. If producers can find a way to share the gains with their retailers, it should be possible to presell a large fraction of products to customers' specifications (at a lower cost and price) while keeping the capability to build customized products (at a higher cost and price) right away for the "got to have it now" customer.

A major challenge to "when it's wanted" consumption is that in complex, multifirm provision streams, the interests of the customer, the retailer, the producer, and the suppliers must be aligned. This brings us to the final principle of lean consumption.

CONTINUALLY AGGREGATE SOLUTIONS TO REDUCE THE CUSTOMER'S TIME AND HASSLE

With our background in lean production, we are repeatedly struck by a phenomenon most business analysts seem to miss: Consumers are using more and more suppliers—frequently strangers reached through impersonal markets—to solve smaller and smaller problems, often on a onetime basis. By contrast, lean producers, following Toyota's example, are steadily reducing their supply base for each item and asking fewer suppliers with deeper knowledge of their needs to solve bigger problems on a continuing basis.

This same concept can be applied to the process of consumption. For example, why can't a single provider solve your computation and communication problems by evaluating your specific needs and then determining the best equipment, software, and services? The provider could then obtain, install, maintain, upgrade, and replace the required items for a standard fee, with no unpaid work or hassle for you. And why can't another solution provider put the vehicles in your driveway, then maintain, repair, and dispose of them as appropriate, for a simple usage fee, without consuming any of your time or attention?

Few such solutions are currently being offered cost effectively for consumers' small number of really big problems: mobility, communication, shelter, health care, financial management, and shopping. (Concierge services and consumer advocates may be available, but are actually a step backward into a world where the well-to-do hire staff to cure their consumption headaches, which are caused by broken processes.)

However, advances in information technology—for managing providers' logistics and connecting consumers and providers—will lift the technical barriers to solving these problems and make solutions cost effective. And transparent pricing of bundled goods and services, along with clear rules governing how providers use consumers' information, will be essential. Finally, providers and consumers will have to truly open lines of communication and learn how to plan together over the long term.

Making Lean Consumption Work

We believe that consumers will be quick to learn their role in lean consumption. Most of us would surely embrace the opportunity to solve our consumption problems completely, getting just what we want, when we want it, where we want it, at an attractive price from a small number of stable providers, with no waste of our time, and with no unpaid work.

The real challenge lies with the retailers, service providers, manufacturers, and suppliers that are not used to looking at total cost from the standpoint of the consumer and are even less accustomed to working with customers to optimize the process of consuming. Lean production has clearly triumphed over similar obstacles in recent years to become the dominant global model. Can lean consumption, its logical companion, be far behind?

Solving Problems at the Source

FUJITSU SERVICES IS ONE OF THE LARGEST providers of IT services in Europe, the Middle East, and Africa, with 15,400 employees in 30 countries and sales of $4.2 billion in 2004. After providing technical support for its own products for many years, Fujitsu began to offer services to companies that were outsourcing their customer service and technical support activities. Here Fujitsu has often found itself playing the difficult role of mediating between hardware and software vendors and users about the problems the latter encountered. Typically, firms like Fujitsu are paid to respond to user complaints at the lowest cost per complaint handled. This call center model gives firms no reason to reduce the number of complaints received and, indeed, creates a disincentive: If the call volume falls, so does the service company's revenue. Fujitsu approached the problem with a completely different mind-set. It decided to eliminate the root causes of callers' complaints.

When Fujitsu took over the help desk contract in 2001 for BMI (an airline formerly known as BMI British Midland), Fujitsu immediately analyzed the different types of calls coming in from BMI employees. Then it set to work to understand the problems that gave rise to the calls; to track the time and effort required to fix them; and, most important, to measure the impact on the business of failures or delays in doing so. (Note that in this example, the users being helped are BMI employees, such as the check-in staff. Operationally, this works the same way as help lines serving customers at, say, Dell or Microsoft.)

Fujitsu found that more than half the calls to help desks were repeat complaints about recurring problems or repair delays. One of the most common reasons for calls—accounting for 26% of the total—was malfunctioning printers: Ticketing agents kept finding that they couldn't print boarding passes and baggage tags for passengers at check-in. It was immediately apparent that solving the printer problem was critical to the airline's business. Given tight airport security, the inability to print boarding passes and baggage tags that could be scanned at a number of points could cause flights to miss their takeoff slots.

Under BMI's previous contractor, the help desk had struggled to get service technicians to respond more quickly so check-in staff wouldn't keep calling with complaints. Fujitsu's response was to find the most cost-effective way to eliminate the root cause of the printer problem. The answer was to convince BMI senior management to spend money up front to install better printers. As a result, the number of calls about malfunctioning printers was cut by more than 80% within 18 months. This action translated into major savings in flight operations far exceeding the cost of the new printers. In addition, Fujitsu improved the technician-response process so that the average time needed to fix printers that still failed fell from ten hours to three.

Fujitsu coupled this problem-solving approach with a different business proposition for BMI. Instead of being paid for each call handled, Fujitsu asked to be paid a set fee based on the number of *potential* callers to the BMI system. This allowed Fujitsu to profitably offer BMI a lower bid than its current vendor.

By addressing root causes, Fujitsu reduced total calls to the help desk by 40% within 18 months and improved customer satisfaction. As the company has pro-gressively applied this problem-solving approach to all of its customers, it has moved beyond its original role as a mediator between vendors and frustrated con-sumers to become an analyst and optimizer of entire IT response systems. Fujitsu is solving the customer's prob-lem completely—and then some.

While discussing a customer's current problem, for example, Fujitsu personnel pass on new information about the user's computing systems, including how to prevent problems the customer hasn't yet encountered but will, if not warned. At the same time, Fujitsu can learn more about what problems the customer is trying to solve with the system, which can lead to ideas for new prod-ucts. Instead of simply fixing defects so that customers get the value originally promised, Fujitsu creates *new* value by offering them additional information and ser-vices they might want. What starts as a negative cus-tomer interaction can turn into an opportunity for informa-tion sharing that builds loyalty, generates fresh market intelligence, and saves Fujitsu money. As a result, satis-fied clients have rewarded Fujitsu with extra work previ-ously divided among competing subcontractors—a win-win for both parties.

Locating for Lean Provision

FROM THE LEAN PERSPECTIVE, the stampede to out-source manufacturing to China in order to serve North American and European customers is questionable, but not for the reasons usually cited. The real challenge for lean providers is the inability of remote production facilities to respond instantly to changing customer demands, such as a surge in requests for size nine gray "Wonder Wings."

Most manufacturers and their retail partners seem to have no method for calculating total costs of the entire provision stream for their products. These include costs for parts, actual logistics (not just the cheap container shipping probably called for in the business plan), stock-outs, remaindering, and carrying inventory over extended supply lines. In our experience, when all these costs are added up to accurately calculate total product costs, the lowest-cost location for labor-intensive products with unpredictable demand is often at the lowest wage point within the region of sale. That means Mexico for North America, Romania and Turkey for Western Europe, and, yes, China for Japan, because rapid replenishment at reasonable cost is possible from these locations.

For lean thinkers, the general rule is that shipping by boat is cheap but slow and, when forecasts are wrong, must be replaced by airfreight that is fast but expensive. By contrast, trucks are much faster than boats and much cheaper than planes. They permit overnight replenishment through each of the loops in a typical provision stream, provided that production is within the geographic region of sale. If you can't eliminate costly activities within production processes, you may still need to relocate to low-wage countries—but do it in a way that minimizes total costs.

In the case of products that are made to order, it might make sense to move manufacturing closer still to the customer, even when that's not the lowest wage point in the region. Consider Nike's surprising approach to the low-cost manufacture of customized goods. On Nike's Web site, you can customize a bag or backpack, choosing from a variety of fabrics and colors for the bag's panels, and even have Nike embroider a monogram or personal message on the item you order. And your customized bag will cost only $10 more (including express shipping) than a standard version in a retail store.

What you wouldn't have known is that your bag will be manufactured to your precise order at NuSewCo, a small contractor in the San Francisco area. At $15 per hour, NuSewCo's labor costs are 20 times higher than the fully loaded labor costs of the contractors in China that make Nike's other products. But Nike calculates that the total expense of obtaining its customized bags using high-priced American labor and offering express delivery is lower than the total cost of sourcing its standard bags for American customers from Southeast Asia and selling them through retail.

How can this be? It's possible because sourcing locally and manufacturing only to order permits Nike to leave out a large number of steps in the logistics and sales processes: The storage of items at the plant in Southeast Asia until there is a full container to take to the port. The further storage of the container at the port while shipping awaits a full load for the container ship. The customs processes on both ends. The storage of the items in the distribution center on the U.S. West Coast and the assembly into containers to send to the stores. The *entire cost* of the store. The cost of the inevitable overstocks. The cost of lost sales due to stock-outs. And the cost of remaindering (which sometimes simply means discarding) the items produced on forecast for those customers who never materialized.

As Nike's cost analysis shows, the touch labor is actually a small portion of the total cost of producing and delivering these products, despite their labor intensity. Most of the costs reside in the various overheads at Nike, the management of the many handoffs from production sources on the other side of the world, the large inventories at many points, the retail dealers' overheads, the lost sales from too few goods, and the lost pricing power from too many.

Originally published in March 2005
Reprint R0503C

From Lean Production to the Lean Enterprise

JAMES P. WOMACK AND DANIEL T. JONES

Executive Summary

SINCE THE PUBLICATION of their 1991 book about lean production in the auto industry, *The Machine That Changed the World*, James Womack and Daniel Jones have seen North American and European companies make amazing improvements by implementing lean-production techniques. The authors have realized that linking these individual breakthroughs up and down the value chain, creating a *lean enterprise*, is the next step in achieving superior performance.

The lean enterprise is a group of individuals, functions, and legally separate but operationally synchronized companies that creates, sells, and services a family of products. Few companies have created a lean enterprise, and understandably. Individuals, functions, and companies have needs that conflict with each other and with those of the lean enterprise. The strengths and weaknesses of the German, U.S., and Japanese industrial traditions suggest that trade-offs between these three entities are inevitable.

Womack and Jones believe, however, that the lean enterprise can satisfy these conflicting needs if managers offer career paths that alternate between concentration on a value chain and knowledge building within functions; turn functions into schools; focus companies on a narrower set of tasks; and implement a new code of behavior to overcome the Cold War relations that prevail among companies in most value chains today.

A concerted effort by companies across the industrial landscape to embrace the lean enterprise and find new tasks for excess employees will be superior to any industrial policy that a government could devise.

In our book *The Machine That Changed the World,* we explained how companies can dramatically improve their performance by embracing the "lean production" approach pioneered by Toyota. By eliminating unnecessary steps, aligning all steps in an activity in a continuous flow, recombining labor into cross-functional teams dedicated to that activity, and continually striving for improvement, companies can develop, produce, and distribute products with *half or less* of the human effort, space, tools, time, and overall expense. They can also become vastly more flexible and responsive to customer desires.

Over the past three years, we have helped a variety of North American and European companies implement lean-production techniques and have studied many others that have adopted the approach. We've seen numerous examples of amazing improvements in a *specific* activity in a *single* company. But these experiences have also made us realize that applying lean techniques to discrete activities is not the end of the road. If individual breakthroughs can be linked up and down the value chain to form a continuous *value stream* that creates, sells, and services a family of products, the performance of the whole can be raised to a dramatically higher level. We think that value-creating activities can be joined, but this effort will require a new organizational model: the *lean enterprise.*

As we envision it, the lean enterprise is a group of individuals, functions, and legally separate but operationally synchronized companies. The notion of the value stream defines the lean enterprise. The group's mission is collectively to analyze and focus a value stream so that it does everything involved in supplying a good or service (from development and production to sales and maintenance) in a way that provides maximum value to the customer. The lean enterprise differs dramatically from the much-discussed "virtual corporation," whose members are constantly coming and going. There is no way that such an unstable entity can sustain the collaboration needed to apply lean techniques along an entire value stream.

We do not know of any group of companies that has yet created a lean enterprise, and understandably. Doing so will entail radical changes in employment policies, the role of functions within companies, and the relationships among the companies of a value stream. Managers will have to concentrate on the performance of the enterprise rather than on the performance of individual people, functions, and companies. This is especially important because even though one company will be the "team leader," the enterprise must be unified by shared logic and shared pains and gains.

Admittedly, linking lean activities is difficult. We've been struck repeatedly by how hard it is for managers, accustomed to overseeing discrete functions and narrow activities while looking out for the interests of their own companies, even to see the entire value stream. Why should companies set their sights on the lean enterprise when so many are still struggling to master lean production? Because unless all members of a value stream pull together, it may be impossible for any one member to maintain momentum. (See the sidebar "Lucas: Undermined from Without and Within" at the end of this article.) Even if one member makes a lot of progress in becoming lean, neither that member nor the stream as a whole will reap the full benefits if another member falls short.

The Three Needs

Getting managers to think in terms of the value stream is the critical first step to achieving a lean enterprise. Managers who have taken this first step, however, have often run into stiff resistance from employees and functional units as well as from other companies in the stream. Individuals, functions, and companies have legitimate needs that conflict with those of the value stream. Anyone aspiring to a lean enterprise must first understand these needs and how to satisfy them. (See the sidebar "Chrysler's Next Challenge: Building Lean Enterprises" at the end this article.)

NEEDS OF THE INDIVIDUAL

For most people, having a job is the minimum requirement for self-respect and financial well-being. Thus it is ludicrous to assume that people will identify and orchestrate changes that eliminate their jobs. Because making any process lean immediately creates large numbers of excess workers and then continually reduces the amount of effort needed, the jobs problem is a major obstacle confronting any enterprise that is trying to make a performance leap and then sustain its momentum.

Beyond a job, most of us need a career to give us a sense that we are developing our abilities and are "going somewhere." Also, most of us need a "home" that defines who we are in our work lives. These yearnings can be filled by a function ("I'm an electrical engineer"), by a company ("I'm a Matsushita employee"), or even by a union ("I'm a Steelworker"). But the value stream itself cannot fill these needs for long. While functions and companies endure, an employee's position within a specific value stream is tied to the life of the product.

NEEDS OF FUNCTIONS

In order to use and expand the knowledge of employees, companies must organize this knowledge into functions, such as engineering, marketing, purchasing, accounting, and quality assurance. But functions do much more than accumulate knowledge; they teach that knowledge to those who identify their careers with the function, and they search continually for new knowledge. In the so-called learning organization, functions are where learning is collected, systematized, and deployed. Functions, therefore, need a secure place in any organization.

Because of the required depth of knowledge, the time and effort needed to obtain that knowledge, and its inherent portability (much knowledge can be carried from one employer to another), functional specialists often feel a stronger commitment to their function and its intellectual tradition than they do to either the value stream or the company. But focusing processes, which is the means of making organizations lean, requires a high degree of cross-functional cooperation. It is not surprising, then, that many executives these days view their functions as obstacles.

Some executives and business theorists advocate permanently assigning members of functions to multifunctional teams as the solution to this conflict between function and process. Others propose weakening functions or subsuming the activities of "minor" functions like marketing within product teams. Both solutions may work for a while but will weaken companies in the long run.

NEEDS OF COMPANIES

The narrower the scope of responsibility, the more easily a company can calculate costs and the benefits it generates and see the results of its improvement efforts. Therefore, the value stream should be segmented so that each company is responsible for a narrow set of activities.

Throughout most of industrial history, the value chain has usually been integrated vertically within one company, or one company has dominated the other companies making up the chain. These practices make sense; after all, a company's most basic need is to survive by making an adequate return, and weak links in the chain can be a far greater threat to a company's survival than the vagaries of the end-user market. As a result, companies understandably consider control more important than efficiency or responsiveness. The natural response during hard times is for the strongest company to reintegrate as many activities as it can within its corporate walls or for each company in the value chain to grab as much of the profits or revenues as it can from its neighbors.

Hints from Three Industrial Traditions

Given all these conflicting needs, it is easy to see why few enterprises achieve maximum efficiency, flexibility, and customer responsiveness. Nor is blasting clear the channel—the stated mission of the process-reengineering movement—likely to provide relief for more than a short spell before the conflicting needs of individuals, functions, and companies gum things up again.

In searching for a solution, it's useful to look anew at the three preeminent industrial traditions: the German, the American, and the Japanese. Each has derived different strengths by trying to satisfy the needs of either the function, the individual, or the company. The conventional wisdom has been that the three traditions, whose shortcomings are the product of these unavoidable trade-offs, are mutually exclusive. We disagree. In the course of our extensive research on German, U.S., and Japanese companies, it has occurred to us that there is a fourth approach. We believe that our model of the lean enterprise will satisfy the needs of individuals, functions, *and* companies. The end result will offer greater value to the customer than the existing traditions can.

THE GERMAN TRADITION

The backbone of German industry has been its intense focus on deep technical knowledge organized into rigidly defined functions. Individuals progress in their careers by climbing the functional ladder. And companies strive to defend their positions in a value chain by hoarding proprietary knowledge within their technical functions.

The consequence of this focus has been great technical depth and an ability to compete globally by offering customized products with superior performance. The weakness of the German tradition, strikingly apparent in the 1990s, is its hostility to cross-functional cooperation. Mercedes-Benz, for example, requires three times the number of hours Toyota requires to engineer and manufacture a comparable luxury car, largely because the engineering functions won't talk to each other. Mercedes makes durable, high-performance cars, but with too many labor-intensive loops in the development process and too little attention to manufacturability. The same holds true for almost all German industries, which have discovered that the world will no longer buy enough customized goods at the high prices required to support the system's inherent inefficiency.

THE AMERICAN TRADITION

The individual has always been at the center of U.S. society. At the beginning of this century, the lack of strong functional and craft traditions and the willingness of suppliers to collaborate with assemblers were major advantages in introducing continuous flow and mass production.

But extreme individualism created its own needs. In the postwar era, managers sought portable professional credentials (e.g., an MBA) and generic expertise independent of a particular business (e.g., finance). And rather than stressing cooperation, each company in a value chain, itself acting as an individual, sought to create its own defendable turf.

The consequence was that U.S. industry gradually became as functional as German industry, but self-preservation, rather than a desire for technical knowledge, drove functionalism in the United States. At the same time, the "every company for itself" tendency most evident in hard times greatly reduced the ability of U.S. companies to think together about the entire value stream. Even though the willingness of Americans to innovate by breaking away from employers and traditional intercompany relationships imparts a real advantage today in nascent industries like information processing and biotechnology, this extreme individualism has caused the United States to lose its lead in efficient production.

THE JAPANESE TRADITION

The Japanese have stressed the needs of the company, which is hardly surprising given the centuries-old feudal tradition of obligation between companies and employees and between big companies and their smaller suppliers and distributors. Government policy, with its focus on production rather than individual consumption, has reinforced this emphasis. The enormous benefit of the Japanese tradition has been the ability of big companies to focus on the needs of the entire value stream unimpeded by functional fiefdoms, career paths within functions, and the constant struggles between members of the value stream to gain an advantage over each other.

But such an exclusive focus on the company produces corresponding weaknesses, which have become apparent over time. For example, the technical functions are weak in most Japanese companies despite the overwhelming dominance of engineers in management. Because most engineers have spent practically all their careers on cross-functional teams developing products or improving production processes, they have gotten better and better at applying what they already know. But the creation of new knowledge back in the technical functions has languished. As a result, many Japanese companies (from Toyota in cars to Matsushita in consumer electronics) that prospered by commercializing and incrementally improving well-understood product and process technologies have now largely cleared the shelf of available ideas for generating fundamentally new, innovative products and processes.

Sony is a case in point. The company recently acknowledged that, for the first time in its history, no dramatic product breakthroughs were imminent and that it would try to defend its competitive position by adopting lean techniques to cut costs in its increasingly mature product lines. We applaud, of course, whenever a company adopts lean techniques. However, these should complement rather than substitute for innovation. Sony must address the weakness of its core technical functions in addition to becoming lean.

Another weakness inherent in the Japanese system is that preserving feudal relationships has become more important than responding to shifts in the market. During the last five years, Japanese companies with massive export surpluses should have redeployed production so that their output in a given region corresponded more closely to sales in that region. Instead, constraints on reassigning employees to new enterprises and abandoning traditional second- and third-tier suppliers caused many big companies to invest in additional domestic capacity for making the same families of products. This is why so many companies, including the model company Toyota, found themselves in deep trouble when the yen strengthened.

New Models for Careers, Functions, and the Company

The critical challenge for managers today is to synchronize the needs of the individual, the function, the company, and the value stream in a way that will yield the full benefits of the lean enterprise while actually increasing individual opportunities, functional strength, and the well-being of member companies. Achieving this balance will require new management techniques, organizational forms, and principles of shared endeavor.

ALTERNATING CAREER PATHS

If we have learned anything in recent years about the value stream, it is that individuals must be totally dedicated to a specific process for the value stream to flow smoothly and efficiently. The old division of labor, which shuttled the product from department to department, must give way to a recombination of labor so that fewer workers, organized in focused teams, can expedite the value flow without bottlenecks or queues. Similarly, functional specialists involved in product development must completely focus on their task in a team context.

But there is a problem. The individual facing permanent assignment to a cross-functional team is being asked to abandon his or her functional career path. At the same time, key functions face the loss of power and importance. When both individuals and functions feel threatened by streamlined processes, these processes won't be streamlined for very long.

The solution is a career path that alternates between concentration on a specific value stream (a family of products) and dedicated, intense knowledge building within functions. These functions must include a new process-management function (in place of industrial engineering and quality assurance) that instills a process perspective in everyone from the top to the bottom of the company.

In following this new career path, the individual's know-how will still be growing. But the value stream itself will get his or her undivided attention for extended periods. Making this model work will be the primary task of the human resource function, which is responsible for ensuring that each individual has a coherent career—a key to attracting and retaining employees.

The concept of an alternating career path has nothing to do with matrix organizations, in which everyone has two bosses. In this new model, the process leader rates an individual's performance while an individual is dedicated to a process, but the function head rates performance while the individual is back in the function. The career planner in human resources, the function head, and the process leader decide jointly where the individual should go next.

Honda has embraced this approach in Japan and North America, particularly for engineers. When engineers join Honda, they go through a rotation, common in Japanese companies, that begins with several months on a production line, followed by short stints in marketing, product planning, and sales. Honda's practice then diverges from the Japanese norm of assigning engineers to and keeping them in process teams. At Honda, the young engineer's first extended assignment is on a product-development team, where he or she performs routine engineering calculations. This assignment continues for the life of the development activity, or up to three years.

After this job, the young engineer is assigned to his or her technical specialty within the engineering department to begin a skills-upgrading process. As part of this phase, the individual is assigned to an advanced engineering effort involving a search for new techniques or capabilities that the company wants to master. The engineer is then typically reassigned to a development team for a new product to perform more complex engineering tasks that call on his or her newly acquired knowledge. After this development effort, the engineer goes back to the "home" engineering function to begin another learn-apply-learn cycle.

FUNCTIONS BECOME SCHOOLS

The problem with functions in most companies today is that they perform the wrong tasks. Purchasing should not purchase. Engineering should not engineer. Production should not produce. In the lean enterprise, functions have two major roles. The first is to serve as a school. They should systematically summarize current knowledge, search for new knowledge, and teach all this to their members, who then spend time on value-creating process teams. (See the sidebar "Unipart: Turning Functions into Schools" at the end of this article.)

The second role of functions is to develop guidelines—the best practices—for, say, purchasing or marketing and to draw up a roster of those companies eligible to be long-term partners in the value stream (suppliers, in the case of the purchasing department). With their counterparts in companies up and down the value stream, functions should also develop rules for governing how they will work together to solve problems that span the companies and for establishing behavioral codes so that one company does not exploit another.

So who actually performs the tasks that these functions traditionally handled? Cross-functional product-development and production teams should select suppliers, develop products, and oversee routine production activities. The traditional purchasing department, for example, should define the principles of enduring relationships with suppliers, draw up the roster of eligible suppliers, and strive to improve continuously the performance of every supplier. The product-development team should perform the purchasing department's traditional job of deciding to obtain a specific amount of a specific item at a target price from a specific supplier for the life of the product.

The experience of Nissan's British subsidiary provides a striking example of what can happen when a purchasing department rethinks its mission. Nissan had serious problems during the 1989 production launch of the Primera, its first car designed for the European market, when several suppliers disrupted production by failing to deliver workable parts on time. The normal course of action in Britain would have been to replace the miscreants. Instead, Nissan's British purchasing department teamed up with the Nissan R&D center to place supplier-development teams of Nissan engineers inside each supplier for extended periods to improve their key processes. Nissan's theory was that setting high standards and giving the suppliers advice on how to meet them would produce superior results. Two years later, when Nissan began production of the Micra, a new small car, this approach had transformed these suppliers from the Nissan subsidiary's worst into its best.

What is the role of other functions? Marketing defines principles of enduring relationships with customers and/or distributors and identifies suitable partners. The traditional marketing and sales tasks of specifying the product, taking orders, and scheduling delivery become the work of the product-development and production teams. Engineering defines the best engineering practices, which it teaches to engineers. It also searches for new capabilities, such as new materials to reduce weight in its products. By undertaking such jobs, the engineering function extends the expertise of the discipline by finding ways to overcome the shortcomings of today's products and processes. It can then apply its new knowledge to the next generation of products or to entirely new products. The product-development team performs all routine engineering; it solves problems that have been solved before for similar products.

Finally, a new process-management function (which still does not exist in the vast majority of companies) does three things: it defines the rules for managing cross-functional teams and the continuous flow of production, including quality assurance; it teaches team leaders in product development and production how to apply these rules; and it constantly searches for better approaches. The old departmental structures within production—molding, painting, assembly, quality assurance—disappear into the continuous-flow production teams in charge of making families of products.

While functions become "support" for value-creating process teams, every function paradoxically has a deeper and more coherent knowledge base than was possible when it divided its attention between thinking and doing. Moreover, this knowledge base is more relevant to the company's long-term needs because function members returning from value-creating assignments in the processes bring new questions for the function to answer. Constantly applying knowledge in this way fights the tendency of all intellectual activities to veer off into abstractions when left in isolation.

A SHARPER FOCUS FOR COMPANIES

Most companies today do too much and do much of it poorly. In the world of the lean enterprise, each company in a value stream will tackle a narrower set of tasks that it can do well.

The company that is the assembler, for example, may find that it no longer needs to design or produce any of the major component systems in its product because product development (in collaboration with suppliers and distributors) and final assembly are its real skills. The component-system supplier may discover it no longer needs to make the parts in its systems because design of the complete system (in collaboration with customers and its own suppliers) is its competitive advantage. New companies may emerge to design component systems or make discrete parts and to supply services, like cleaning facilities, that are tangential to the mission of focused companies. Japanese industries, whose companies have been less vertically integrated than U.S. and European companies, have long taken this approach, and many North American and European industries, from aerospace to automotive to appliances, are following suit.

At the same time, all companies will need to participate in several enterprises involving different sets of companies in order to obtain the stability that any one value stream, with its inevitable ups and downs, cannot

provide. Stability aside, companies will want to participate in a range of streams involving a range of products
or services in order to learn from companies that think in
different ways. This is a key to continuous improvement.

A New Code of Behavior

For lean companies to be able to work together and to be
assured of survival, they must develop new principles for
regulating their behavior. Cold War-like relations prevail
among companies in most value chains today. No one
would suggest that the real Cold War would have been
resolved if the Eastern and Western blocs simply trusted
each other. The current notion that companies can end
their hostilities simply by embracing trust is equally
implausible.

All negotiated peace arrangements, including those in
the corporate world, entail an agreement on the principles of just behavior and procedures that enable each
party to verify that others are keeping their end of the
deal. When this latter condition is met, trust occurs naturally because everyone can see what's going on.

Achieving cooperation within the value stream is particularly difficult. Every stream needs a "team leader," a
company that orchestrates the decision to form an enterprise, pulls together the full complement of member
companies, and leads the joint analysis of the total enterprise stream. Unfortunately, industrial history is replete
with stories of companies that have used their leadership
positions to extract advantage from upstream and downstream partners. And the overwhelming expectation is
that these leaders will continue to behave this way.

Obviously, the principles for regulating behavior
within a value stream will vary with the nature of the

product and the degree of familiarity of its member companies. However, there must be clear agreements on target costing (deciding what price the customer would pay for a product and then working backward to determine how that product can be made so that it also delivers a profit), acceptable levels of process performance, the rate of continuous improvement (and cost reductions), consistent accounting systems to analyze costs, and formulas for splitting pain and gain.

In every case, companies in a stream must discuss the total activity, the performance requirements for individual activities, the verification procedures for performance, and the reward formulas. They must do this before they embark on the task and adopt explicit principles of interaction that everyone agrees are just. This is what Nissan is attempting to do.

When Nissan established its manufacturing operation in Britain in 1986, it could not bring most of its suppliers from Japan. (Its production volume was initially too small, and it had agreed to make cars with a high level of local content in return for start-up aid from the British government.) But the European companies that were chosen as suppliers were initially unsure of the depth of Nissan's commitment to them. Would Nissan eventually replace them with members of its own *keiretsu* from Japan? Would the company's commitment to its European suppliers survive the next economic downturn?

To dispel these doubts, Nissan has worked hard to establish and adhere to principles governing its relationships with suppliers. These include a permanent commitment to suppliers that make a continuous effort to improve; a clear role for each supplier within the supply chain; a joint examination of ways the entire value stream can reduce costs; and a commitment to help improve processes when problems emerge. These principles explain Nissan's decision to help inept suppliers improve rather than dumping them, a decision that sent a powerful signal to the rest of its suppliers and strengthened the group's pursuit of the lean enterprise.

Once companies in the stream, including the team leader, accept a set of clear principles, the next step is mutual verification. The activities of each company must be transparent so that the upstream and downstream collaborators can verify that all tasks are being performed adequately. One way to do this is a continuing process "audit" similar in spirit to the audits companies currently perform on the quality assurance techniques of suppliers. Such audits must be conducted jointly and in both directions: customer-supplier and supplier-customer. This means the end of secrecy in product development and production operations and suggests the need to go even further with activity-based costing so that the indirect costs of all activities are fully understood and dramatically reduced.

The most difficult disputes between enterprise members will involve their respective productivity and creativity rather than their respective profit margins. Some members might say to another member, "Your profit margin is actually too low. Your costs are much too high because you failed to apply lean techniques in product development and production processes. We won't help pay for your inefficiency." Or they might say, "You seem unable to provide the next generation of technology for a key component system in our shared product. Address this issue or find a new enterprise!"

Proposals for virtual corporations, in which "plug-compatible" members of the value stream come and go, fail to grasp the massive costs of casual interactions.

These arrangements are fine for nascent industries in which product specification and market demand are subject to dramatic and unpredictable change. But they are terrible for the vast majority of commercial activities.

The lean enterprise is also very different from the vertical keiretsu of Japan, whose members cement their relationships by taking equity stakes in each other. Unlike keiretsu members, participants in the lean enterprise must be free to leave if collaborators fail to improve their performance or refuse to reveal their situation.

Strategy for the Lean Enterprise

The companies joined in a lean enterprise must target the best opportunities for exploiting their collective competitive advantage. But their strategic thinking must also include a new element to complement and sustain the new concepts of careers, functions, companies, and the shared enterprise: how to find additional activities sufficient in magnitude to sustain the relationships that are the basis of superior performance.

We noted at the outset that, by its nature, the lean enterprise does more and more with less and less. This performance leap requires the continuing gung-ho involvement of every employee and allied company. All companies in a value stream must collectively determine how much labor, space, tooling, and time are necessary. Each member of the enterprise must then focus its activities by returning all employees who are not creating value to their home functions. It is impossible to implement and sustain a lean value stream with excess people, space, time, and tools.

Of course, unceremoniously dumping employees and allies as productivity gains are realized is the best way to ensure that such gains are not sustained. Employees will naturally place self-preservation above the value stream. In addition, companies that fire thousands of people run the risk of sparking a public backlash that could lead to greater government restrictions on their ability to shrink their workforces.

So how can companies avoid massive layoffs? One way is lowering prices by passing the cost savings on to the final consumer in order to increase sales or to grab share from less lean competitors. (Obviously, individual suppliers, especially in the West, now cannot dictate that their price reductions be passed on to final consumers. This is another reason the lean enterprise, which can make sure this happens, is so important.) Another way is speeding up product development to expand offerings in existing product families and to create new markets for core technologies.

Clearly, not every company in every enterprise can preserve all of its jobs. Some companies in mature industries may have to lay off workers or abandon suppliers. However, companies that sincerely and visibly explore all options for preserving jobs as they create lean enterprises will make unavoidable layoffs easier for employees to accept.

The Prize

A concerted effort by companies across the industrial landscape to embrace the lean enterprise *and* find new tasks for excess employees will be vastly superior to any industrial policy that governments devise. An economy dominated by lean enterprises continually trying to improve their productivity, flexibility, and customer responsiveness might finally be able to avoid the kind of social upheavals that have occurred when new production systems have rendered existing ones obsolete.

If this sea change in industrial practice comes to pass, most individuals, companies, and enterprises will prosper. Equally important, we will witness a productivity explosion, coupled with employment stability, that will provide the long-sought antidote to the economic stagnation plaguing all advanced economies.

Lucas: Undermined from Without and Within

BY IMPLEMENTING LEAN TECHNIQUES, Lucas PLC, a British supplier of mechanical and electrical components to the automotive and aerospace industries, made great strides in improving product quality and on-time deliveries. But after about seven years, progress ground to a halt in some operations because key customers had not similarly adopted lean thinking. And other operations began to backslide as Lucas's plant managers and functional departments resisted changes that they saw as threats to their power.

Lucas was one of the first British companies to adopt lean techniques when it recruited University of Birmingham Professor John Parnaby in 1983 to head a new process-improvement function. Parnaby quickly introduced the concepts of the Toyota Production System throughout Lucas, with extremely promising initial results. For example, a Lucas aerospace-component plant halved its lead times and work-in-progress inventories, and a truck-component plant doubled its inventory turns and boosted the portion of orders delivered on time from

25% to 98%. Thanks to such improvements, Lucas began to overcome its reputation among customers as the "Prince of Darkness."

But problems soon emerged. An electrical-component factory that had embraced lean techniques, for example, found itself backsliding because big customers like Rover and Ford had not yet made their operations lean. As a result, these customers continued to place orders in an unpredictable fashion. To cope, the factory had to maintain relatively high inventories, a cardinal sin in lean production. True to form, workers began to rely on the inventories as a safety net, and the lean factory began to gain weight.

Within Lucas, the new process-improvement function was soon locked in a struggle with the traditional, vertical functions—marketing, product development, engineering, and production—over the former's efforts to improve efficiency. One plant installed a production line to manufacture a mechanical system in a continuous flow. But ignoring Parnaby's protests, the engineering function bought and installed some expensive, inflexible machines, which, as is typical of such equipment, were difficult to switch from making one type of component to making another. As a result, the plant had to revert to batch production, and inventories and inefficiencies quickly increased.

Internal conflict at Lucas was also evident at a plant for making truck components when the product-design function refused the advice of the process-management function. The latter developed a component that promised to be superior to competitors' offerings, but it turned out that the component couldn't be manufactured to the tolerances required. If a cross-functional design team including process management and production engineering had overseen the project, this folly could have been avoided.

Discouraged by all the battles within and without, Parnaby scaled back his efforts to institute lean thinking at Lucas. Hard hit by slumps in its key markets in the 1990s, Lucas has seen its profits wither, has suffered from management turmoil, and has dramatically shrunk its product offerings and slashed its payrolls. The company has also been a rumored takeover target. The person who must contend with these problems is George Simpson, who will assume the helm of Lucas in May. As the chairman of Rover, the British automaker, Simpson has used lean production to improve Rover's competitiveness dramatically. He will undoubtedly try to force Lucas to carry on the lean revolution it began over a decade ago.

Chrysler's Next Challenge: Building Lean Enterprises

AS WE WERE FINISHING OUR RESEARCH for *The Machine That Changed the World* in early 1990, we decided to say as little about Chrysler as possible. We believed that the company's managers were brilliant at selling poor-quality products and terrible at product development, production operations, and supply-chain management. While Chrysler executives vowed that they were implementing lean techniques in each of these areas, we were highly skeptical.

We were spectacularly wrong. Chrysler actually was embracing lean production, and the company is now trying to turn the value chains it leads into lean enterprises. As Chrysler has worked toward this end, the conflicts between the needs of value streams and those of the individuals, functions, and companies that make up the streams have become fully apparent. Chrysler is beginning to realize that overcoming these obstacles is its next great challenge.

As part of Chrysler's move toward lean production, the company revamped its purchasing system and deployed cross-functional "platform" teams, each of which focuses on developing one line of cars or trucks. The platform teams have been a spectacular success in part because Chrysler appointed a traditional function head to lead each team in order to minimize process-function conflict. The head of purchasing, for example, also heads the small-car team. Therefore, if a function acts as a roadblock to one platform team, the team's leader can threaten to hold hostage the product under development by the offending function head's own team. We don't propose this as a model for other companies, but this approach has certainly ended Chrysler's long-standing functional feuding.

Thanks to a host of new products that command prices in the top range of their market segments and dramatic reductions in production costs due to better design, Chrysler will probably make as much money in 1994 as will all Japanese automakers combined. Moreover, the time that Chrysler requires to bring a product concept to market has been cut from 60 months in the 1980s to 31 months for the Neon, launched in January 1994. The number of full-time engineers involved in developing a new body and integrating the vehicle systems has gone from 1,400 to 700. And the enhanced manufacturability of the product has reduced the number of hours required to paint, weld, and assemble a vehicle from 35 to 22. Both the amount of time spent on final tinkering with the product in the early stages of production and the number of product recalls have also been slashed.

But such successes do not mean all is well. Most members of the platform teams have been permanently removed from their former functional "home," the body engineering department. Until recently, team members were content to be part of a process with clear and positive results. But they are now becoming anxious about their lack of a career path (these teams don't need layers of managers with fancy titles) and the dilution of their skills due to lack of communication with colleagues elsewhere in the company. Chrysler's challenge is to define a new career for these employees, which should involve alternating them between teams engaged in developing and making products and jobs where they can deepen their skills.

Such a solution would also address an emerging problem caused by the elimination of the body engineering department. While this department was a major roadblock for the company, its elimination has created a vacuum in functional expertise at a time when the auto industry is experimenting with new body technologies based on aluminum space frames with plastic or aluminum skins. Chrysler dares not fall behind in its fundamental technical capabilities but does not wish to send the advanced R&D function on excursions unrelated to the practical needs of the platform teams. The company, therefore, must redefine its engineering functions so that they support its key processes but still have a life of their own.

Chrysler also faces the challenge of redefining its supplier relations in order to create four lean enterprises: small cars, large cars, minivans, and trucks and Jeeps. The company has winnowed its supplier base from a chaotic mass of 2,500 in the late 1980s to a lean, long-term nucleus of 300. At the moment, suppliers love working for Chrysler, and for obvious reasons: the company's production volume is growing rapidly. Chrysler includes suppliers in development activities from day one and listens eagerly to their suggestions for design improvements and cost reductions. Chrysler has also replaced its adversarial bidding system with one in which the company designates suppliers for a component and then uses target pricing (figuring out how much consumers will pay for a vehicle and then working backwards to divvy up the costs and profits) to determine with suppliers the component prices and how to achieve them. Most parts are sourced from one supplier for the life of the product.

Despite these improvements, Chrysler still pays too much for most of its parts. The problem is not excessive supplier profit margins but that Chrysler, like most Western automakers, has not been successful in getting suppliers to implement lean techniques in ways that are best for the enterprise. In addition, Chrysler and its suppliers have yet to devise pain-sharing principles to keep their relationship from degenerating into an "every company for itself" battle in the next economic downturn.

Chrysler's management is energetically trying to address these problems. Indeed, Chairman Robert Eaton and President Robert Lutz have made it clear that Chrysler's main challenge in the 1990s is devising and perfecting its own lean enterprises.

Unipart: Turning Functions into Schools

BRITAIN'S UNIPART GROUP has gone further than most companies in turning its functions into schools as part of the company's effort to become lean. Unipart was created in 1987, when Rover sold a collection of disparate, highly autonomous functions to employees. Unipart then turned these functions into independent divisions, which included auto-parts manufacturing; warehousing, distribution, marketing, and sales of Unipart's and others' auto components; information systems; and video production.

John Neill, Unipart's CEO, pushed each Unipart business to become lean on its own. But auto-parts manufacturing was clearly the most successful. Its plants that make fuel tanks and exhaust systems for cars, which learned lean techniques from Honda's and Toyota's British plants, won the U.K. Factory of the Year Award in 1989 and 1993.

When Neill decided that the auto-parts manufacturing business should teach the other businesses its secrets, he quickly realized that given their history of operating autonomously, this was much easier said than done. He also realized that if things did not change, Unipart would fail to leverage the knowledge of a practice leader, and, because the businesses were interdependent to a certain extent, the laggards would prevent the whole company from becoming as lean as possible.

To tackle these problems, Neill created "Unipart University." He made each business responsible for finding the best practice in its field, customizing it for Unipart, and then teaching it to the other businesses and their partners. In other words, each Unipart business, complete with its own "faculty," is a center of expertise. "Through this forum we share the best available learning with our colleagues," Neill says.

The Information Technology Faculty, which resides in the information-systems company, for example, is responsible for upgrading IT skills throughout Unipart. And the

Industries Faculty, which resides in the manufacturing company, is playing the lead role in teaching its suppliers as well as the warehouse operation the process-management techniques it gleaned from Honda and Toyota. In the case of the warehouse operation, this entails teaching it how to work with its major suppliers so that together they can fill orders on time, which will enable the warehouse operation to cut its inventories.

The "deans" of the faculties, most of whom are the heads of the businesses, sit on the Deans Group, which steers the university, ensures that problems are discussed companywide, and initiates research on ways to solve them. The Deans Group recently charged two faculties with a critical task: researching how to select and develop leaders of self-managed, shop-floor teams. As part of that effort, the group from the industries and warehousing faculties visited Japan and the United States as well as Honda's and Toyota's British operations.

"Our vision," Neill says, "is to build the world's best lean enterprise. That means continuously integrating training, or should I say learning, into the decision-making systems of the company."

Originally published in March–April 1994
Reprint 94211

About the Contributors

PAUL S. ADLER is a professor at the University of Southern California School of Business Administration.

CARLISS Y. BALDWIN is the William L. White Professor of Business Administration at the Harvard Business School in Boston, Massachusetts.

H. KENT BOWEN is a professor emeritus focusing in the field of operations and technology management at Harvard Business School.

KIM B. CLARK is President of Brigham Young University–Idaho. Until 2005, he was Dean of Harvard Business School.

DANIEL T. JONES is the chairman of the Lean Enterprise Academy in Herefordshire, England.

JEFFREY K. LIKER is Professor of Industrial and Operations Engineering at the University of Michigan in Ann Arbor and principle of Optiprise, Inc.

ANAND P. RAMAN is senior editor, *Harvard Business Review*.

DURWARD K. SOBEK II is an assistant professor of mechanical and industrial engineering at Montana State University in Bozeman.

STEVEN J. SPEAR is an assistant professor of business administration at Harvard Business School in Boston.

THOMAS A. STEWART is editor of *Harvard Business Review.*

KATSUAKI WATANABE is the president of Toyota Motor Corporation.

ALLEN C. WARD is an adjunct researcher at the University of Michigan and the president of Ward Synthesis, an engineering consulting company in Ann Arbor.

JAMES P. WOMACK is the founder and chairman of the Lean Enterprise Institute in Brookline, Massachusetts.

Index